LEAD CHANGE
without
LOSING IT

✴ ✴ ✴ ✴ ✴

Five Strategies That Can
REVOLUTIONIZE
How You Lead Change
When Facing Opposition

CAREY NIEUWHOF

RETHINK

ENDORSEMENTS

"*Leading Change Without Losing It* is a practical guide to help church leaders of every kind navigate change in the face of opposition. Because so many church leaders are trying to transition an existing ministry rather than start a new one, this book comes at a critical time. The five strategies Carey outlines are practical and applicable to virtually any organization."
Andy Stanley, Senior Pastor, North Point Ministries

"If you lead in the church, you need this book. Leading through change is an inevitable part of church ministry and how you navigate these difficult waters will many times determine the legacy that you leave."
Pete Wilson, Pastor, Cross Point Church, author of Plan B, *co-author of* Empty Promises

"Every leader—myself included—knows *what* we need to change. We get stuck at *how* to bring about change. I made a long list of leaders I know who need to read *Leading Change Without Losing It*. Carey Nieuwhof is both deep and practical—an unbeatable combination."
Kara Powell, Executive Director, Fuller Youth Institute, co-author of Sticky Faith

"Knowing Carey Nieuwhof personally makes this book even better than it already is. He has produced a masterpiece to help young leaders like me not completely blow it when it comes to leading through change. I'm buying cases for our team and clients!"
Casey Graham, Co-founder, Giving Rocket and Preaching Rocket

"When I first started reading Carey's book, I thought I was doing so for Carey. I believe in him, have enjoyed his posts and prior work, and have always found him to be helpful and intentional in his writings. If Carey wanted me to read his new book, why would I say no? Then I started reading. Wow! Did he write this for me? I realized that Carey was addressing many of the issues I am about to face in a job transition. I'm going to face opposition to what I sense God is calling me to do. Carey's book gave me new encouragement, even before I pursue my next God-given dream. Something tells me, this book is going to have the same impact on you. Read this book!"
Ron Edmondson, pastor, leadership consultant, and blogger

"Carey is an incredible leader who has an uncanny gift for articulating difficult issues and providing practical solutions. Every great leader has faced tremendous opposition when pursuing a dream, and Carey has done a brilliant job of providing clear steps that every leader would be wise to follow."
Joe Sangl, President and CEO, Injoy Stewardship Solutions

"Leading through change is one of the most important, and one of the most challenging, calls any Christian leader will ever face. In *Leading Change Without Losing It* Carey Nieuwhof provides you with the inspiration you'll need to stay the course, but more importantly with practical tools you'll need to complete the task."
W. Scott Cochrane, Executive Director, The Leadership Centre Willow Creek Canada

COPYRIGHT

LEADING CHANGE WITHOUT LOSING IT

Published by The reThink Group, Inc.
5870 Charlotte Lane, Suite 300
Cumming, GA 30040 U.S.A.

reThink and The reThink Group logo are registered trademarks of
The reThink Group, Inc.

Scripture quotation (in Introduction of this book) taken from the Holy Bible,
King James Version, Cambridge, 1769.

Scripture marked "NIV" is taken from the Holy Bible, NEW INTERNATION-
AL VERSION®. Copyright © 1973, 1978, 1984 by Biblica, Inc. All rights
reserved worldwide. Used by permission.

Scripture quotations marked NLT are taken from the Holy Bible, New Living Translation, copyright © 1996, 2004. Used by permission of Tyndale
House Publishers, Inc., Wheaton, Illinois 60189. All rights reserved.

ISBN 978-0-9854116-5-7

Edited by Melanie Williams
Cover design by Jim Krause
Interior illustration by Jodi Blackwell
Additional design by Mike Davis

Printed in the United States of America
First Edition 2012
1 2 3 4 5 6 7 8 9 10
082412

DEDICATION

To my family: my wife, Toni, and my sons, Jordan and Sam. Because you've lived and even thrived on the inside of the change.

CONTENTS

FOREWORD

If you are a church leader, then sooner or later you will be required to lead change. Any church that embraces a calling to make disciples in a complex culture will be compelled to consistently rethink and re-evaluate how they do what they do. Remember, it's not your programs or methods as a church that are sacred; it's your mission. So read this book carefully. Carey has navigated the waters of change and has seasoned insights on how to transform your church to reach this generation.

The first time I met Carey Nieuwhof, he was hosting a conference to challenge churches in his denomination to make radical changes. Since then, Carey's story has unfolded to be an incredible illustration of how to lead change. He is a unique leader. He has an uncompromising passion to make people who are outside the church walls a priority. Carey is obsessed with a concept of the Great Commission that puts the mission of Jesus Christ ahead of religious preference and tradition.

Whoever leads a church to make meaningful change can expect a host of obstacles and personal critics. So *Leading Change Without Losing It* is one of the best road maps I know of to help you restyle your ministry. Almost every week a leader will ask me this question, "What are the keys to effectively transitioning a church?" My answer until now has been, "You need to talk to Carey Nieuwhof." From now on, my first response will be, "Have you spent time discussing *Leading Change* with your staff?" I genuinely believe reading this book could make the difference in whether or not your church becomes a relevant influence in your community.

Reggie Joiner, Founder & President, Orange

PREFACE

This is definitely a "they never taught me this in seminary" kind of book. And even if you've never been to seminary, I'm pretty sure no one covers this in staff or volunteer orientation either. (If they did, you might decide to step back on Day 1. Which, come to think of it, might be why nobody teaches this stuff in advance.)

But it's a subject that all of us encounter, sometimes immediately, and definitely within a year of assuming leadership of any kind. You necessarily run into it if you have any amount of passion around your vision—your dream—for what you hope to accomplish in ministry (or, better put, what you pray God will accomplish through you).

Dreamers always try to bring about change. And dreamers almost always encounter opposition. That's what this book and **THE TWO THAT WILL FOLLOW IT*** are about.

I learned many great things through my training for ministry, but I'm not sure we even had one 10-minute conversation about how to navigate change, or opposition to change, as a leader. Maybe that explains why this subject catches most of us off guard and unprepared.

The teachings in this trilogy of books on change are the lessons learned from over 15 years of leading in the local church. Some principles you will recognize. Others might be new and even surprising, but I hope they will affirm what your intuition has always sensed to be the right approach, even if you weren't sure you should act on it. Regardless, I hope they will be helpful. It is possible to lead change without losing it. At least that's what I've experienced personally.

My particular context is this: I've been a senior pastor in the same region north of Toronto, Canada for over 15 years. It was not what I thought I would end up doing with my life. Strangely, I decided when I was eight years old that I wanted to be a lawyer (what kind of eight-year-old wants to be a lawyer?). I chased that dream and eventually got into the law school I wanted to attend. During law school, two things happened: I met my wife (which was awesome!) and sensed, for the first time in my life, a call into ministry (which was confusing).

I finished up law school, got called to the bar, and, trying to be obedient, started months later in seminary, still trying to figure out what this calling meant. Wondering if the calling might be congregational ministry, our young family moved from Toronto an hour north to Central Ontario, where I started serving three small, rural Presbyterian congregations as a student pastor. I was trying to figure out what it meant to be a pastor, and they were trying to figure out what it meant to be the church. In many ways, it was a great match.

The churches were very traditional, each over 100 years old, with small buildings and small numbers. The average attendance at one church was six. Not 60. Six (including low-flying aircraft). Adding all three churches together, the average combined attendance was 50. The combined budgets of the three churches totaled just over $40,000 per year.

We sat down around the leadership table together and began to talk, read our Bibles, and pray. In the first seven years, we navigated the following changes:

- We changed our style of worship from very traditional to a very "contemporary" style (that sounds so … dated, but what else do you call it?).

- We moved from an insider focus to a focus on outsiders we needed to reach.

- We reprogrammed all the ministries and stopped doing things like potlucks, bake sales, bazaars, and fundraisers so we could focus on ministry.

- We sold all three historic buildings and became a new church with a new mission, a new name, and a new place.

- After a few years in an elementary school, we moved into a new $2.1 million facility.

- We remodeled our governance and moved toward a staff-led model.

To be truthful, there was almost nothing we didn't change. And in just over 10 years, we grew from 50 in worship to 800.

Despite the incredible experiences we had shared, a number of us felt a prompting to change once again. For a variety of reasons (and I'm certainly not saying this is something others should do; it's just what I felt I needed to do), in 2007, I left the denomination, and together with an incredible team of people, launched a new church, Connexus, with campuses both north and south of where we used to be located.

It's quite a change, moving from a permanent, nearly paid-for facility, to starting all over with zero dollars and a dream of reaching more unchurched people, in a multi-site portable model of church, but we did. Four years later, almost a thousand now come to our campuses on a Sunday, over half of whom were not churchgoers before they came to Connexus.

That's a bit of change over the last 15 years. And while I would go through it all again in a heartbeat, it didn't come without some opposition. It's out of those experiences and lessons that this book has been written. My hope is that it (and all the books in this series) will encourage and connect a community of us who are living through deep internal and external changes. I hope we can learn from each other. I've discovered that "change stories" have a way of uniting almost any group of church leaders, regardless of denomination, geography, or background.

I also hope these books help fill a bit of a gap. The majority of conferences, books, and seminars in the church world are usually produced by people who started churches. Don't get me wrong: I love church planters, and having planted a church now as well, I have a huge appreciation for the church planting movement in North America and around the world.

But it's always struck me as ironic that while the majority of conferences, books, and seminars are hosted or written by church planters, close to 90% of the people who attend these conferences and read these books are actually leaders who are trying to *transition* existing churches. Having been in both worlds of church transitioning and church planting, I hope this book speaks into the reality of everyone who is trying to effect change, be it in a young church plant or a 150-year-old congregation.

It is possible to lead change without losing it. And my hope is that a generation of leaders will not just learn that, but live it. If this book helps in any way with that, I will be very grateful.

INTRO

DON'T DIE TO YOUR DREAM

Pro cycling may not be everybody's thing, but watching the final day of the Tour de France is incredibly inspiring, as the riders cross into Paris and pedal hard to the finish line at the Champs-Élysées. Okay, maybe not as inspiring as a seconds-to-go, come-from-behind Super Bowl win. Or a walk-off-home-run-to-end-the-ninth Game 7 of the World Series. But if you're a spandex-wearing cyclist like I am (yes, I'm one of those people) who loves to bike (even poorly), there's a level of respect there that runs deep.

Lance Armstrong captured people's imaginations a number of years ago with his unprecedented seven Tour wins. He had a dream of not just winning the Tour, but to win it more times than any other person had won it, and all that *after* beating cancer.

He didn't win seven times without some opposition. They call the Tour de France one of the most grueling races on the planet. The final day of the race, a relatively easy spin into historic Paris, is actually the culmination of almost 3,500 km (over 2,100 miles) in 20+ days of biking in which riders race through the mountains on at least nine days.

Mountains. As in the Alps.

I have trouble with the hill near my house.

Tour de France riders burn about 10,000 calories a day and ride at average speeds of 39 km/hr (24 miles an hour). On a bike. That you pedal. Oh, and they ride up to six hours a day for three weeks, with only two rest days the entire race.

So when they cruise to victory, it masks how hard these guys have had to work to even finish the race, let alone win it. They battle wind, rain, cobblestone streets, mountains, each other, and, most of all, themselves.

But that's what it takes to see the challenge through, right? Although the Tour de France might be an extreme example, there is no victory without struggle, no triumph without some kind of opposition. Any dream comes with opposition.

And so does yours.

DREAMER

As a leader, you have a dream. Every leader has one. It's a picture of a better future, a tomorrow that doesn't look nearly as frustrating or flat-lined as today does.

Like you, I have some dreams. I dream of being a better husband and father; I dream of a church that reaches thousands of unchurched people; I dream of a staff that is energized not only by their calling but by their work environment. I dream of every family making it through whatever turbulence they're facing and placing Jesus at the center of their lives. I dream of helping other people accomplish their dreams.

So do you. Your dream fuels you. You are *excited* by the change you want to usher in, whatever that change is. Whether it's doing a better job reaching new families, changing up your current roster of ministry programs, reorganizing your staff and volunteers, launching a new idea you dreamed up, creating a stronger presence in your community, or—just maybe—leading a complete transformation of the ministry you're a part of, you have a dream.

Your dream necessarily involves change: moving from what is to what could be. And that's appropriate. After all, to some extent that's what godly leaders are called to do—effect necessary and life-transforming change. Think of Moses leading the people through the wilderness, Joseph saving the nation of Israel from famine, David building a city and nation, and the Apostle Paul blazing trails for the early church; God inspires visions. Like the one you believe He has given you. Leaders rarely imagine spending their lives curating the status quo. Because you are passionate about the vision for change you believe God has birthed in your heart, you anticipate that when you introduce that change, the waters will part, just like they did for Moses. At least that's what you think. Or hope. Or dream.

Maybe the picture you have of how the change is going to unfold looks like this: You announce the change. People immediately see the wisdom of it, stand up, and applaud wildly. You implement it. And everyone lives happily ever after. Isn't that, after all, how change is supposed to happen?

SOMETIMES IT FEELS LIKE A BAD DREAM

The only problem is that it almost *never* works out that way. In fact, at some point, almost every dream begins to feel like a nightmare. You hardly need to get out of the gate to discover resistance. Just hint at change and you will discover that you have opposition. Simply pulling out a paintbrush to freshen that dingy hallway in the preschool wing can push someone's buttons. Usher in a new direction for music at your church and you'll discover a number of people who are ready to usher you in a new direction—out the door. Not only do you wonder where God is in the mix, you spend hours trying to remember why you wanted to do this in the first place.

It seems that few of us are exempt. Change challenges assumptions, and people react when assumptions are challenged. James (not his real name) is a student ministry leader in the northeastern United States who discovered the hard way just how angry people can get. James and a group of high school students were heading back one night from an event when one of the students said he thought it was wrong for blacks to marry whites. Deciding he would challenge some assumptions, James simply asked the student why he believed that. It led to a great and healthy discussion about biblical values, equality, and why people believe what they believe.

After that ride home, an upset mother, who was a regular at the church, complained to the senior pastor. Instead of making an appointment, she simply parked her car behind the senior pastor's vehicle, marched inside, and made it clear she wasn't leaving until the senior pastor heard her out.

As James tells it, he had hoped the senior pastor would call him in to hear the other side of the story and resolve the issue. He never did. In fact, the few voices raised in complaint against James kept at it until James became uncomfortable enough with the unresolved conflict that he began to reconsider his ministry there. He and his wife had just purchased a house in the community a few months before. Listen to James as he finishes the story:

> **As we knew the growing swell of negativity was attacking us and the pastor wasn't standing by us, we did not have confidence to sign the mortgage when the house was completed. We had been praying over the house as it was built, dedicating it to God, and dreaming of having students over regularly and someday having our own babies in it. As the house was drawing closer to completion and all this negativity was growing against us, we had no confidence the church would keep us, and we'd be stuck. We asked to have one more meeting with the pastor to ask what he thought about us long-term. He loved what we were doing, but admitted he didn't know what to do about complaining people and didn't want to lose them. My wife and I looked at each other sitting with him in the empty student ministry room and knew we needed to offer to quit. The pastor cried and said he was sorry.**

Welcome to the world of leading change. Fortunately, James went on to do student ministry in another, healthier church, but the wounds remain (not to mention the problems at the original church). But James' story is hardly unique. A RECENT STUDY[1] showed that 25% of all pastors are likely to be fired at some point because of opposition in the church—and that doesn't count those who resign or simply give up.

Not only do leaders lose their jobs over change, something worse happens: leaders lose heart when their hopes for change die. You've seen it and I've seen it. Leaders who used to be optimistic, passionate, and excited enter several rounds of attempted change and emerge cynical, defeated, and jaded. You don't want to be that person, but even as you read this, you might realize that you're on the edge of becoming that person.

It affects all leaders in significant ways. Senior pastors and leaders carry the weight of the entire organization—the expectations of the elders, the board, the staff, the long-time members, and the people you want to reach. You want to change, but there are so many stakeholders you just can't ignore.

Leaders who don't hold the most senior position find a different kind of challenge. Your vision might not align with the senior leader's vision, plus you have all the other stakeholders around you as well. Many secondary leaders, and even volunteers, feel the frustration of having accomplished all the change they can within their sphere but hitting a glass ceiling when they can't convince the senior leader or governing board that further change is needed. Opposition comes in many forms.

The hard reality is that if you attempt to change almost anything, you will encounter resistance. Some of that is natural. Before judging others for their resistance to change, just try changing something in your own life, even something that's 100% within your control, like losing 10 pounds. There's a part of your mind that is absolutely determined to lose weight. Then there's the other part. Inevitably, the part of your mind in favor of change is challenged by the part that is hungry, tired, and fully convinced that you don't really need to change your eating habits and this whole idea is inconvenient, unnecessary, and even impossible.

If none of us needs to step out of our own skin to encounter resistance, why should we be surprised that when we ask others to change, we meet opposition? If we can't even change our own lives without adversity, why would we think leading others through change would be any simpler?

WHAT'S AT STAKE

As challenging as change might be, it's critical that we figure out how to navigate it. A few years ago I was at a graveside service for someone I knew. As the service wrapped up and people started drifting away, a headstone caught my eye. I'm always interested in what people write on their tombstones. It's rather intimidating to think your entire life can be summed up in a phrase or quotation.

This one grabbed me because it was a Bible verse, but not a typical Psalm 23 or John 14 quotation. In fact, it snared my attention because I'd never seen it on a tombstone before. It simply said:

> "Go ye into all the world and preach the gospel to every creature." Mark 16:15

I felt genuinely inspired. I thought, "That's the kind of verse I want on my tombstone." I found myself wanting to know the story of the person who was buried there. Who was this guy? Did I know his family or his kids? What kind of life did he live? How long ago did he live?

As I moved around to read the front of the stone, I was stunned by what I saw. The gravestone wasn't for a person. It was for a *church*. A church that had closed 30 years prior.

I remembered then the story of this church. People from the community had told me about it over the years. At one point it had a vibrant witness, but after the Second World War it began to shrink, until finally in the early 1970s there were not enough people left to make it viable. They closed the doors, tore the building down, and—as I discovered—erected a tombstone that memorialized the importance of preaching the Gospel.

How sadly ironic. A tombstone for a church that failed to change.

I'm worried that more epitaphs like this will be written unless we learn to navigate change better. We don't just need to develop a desire to change; we need to figure out how to lead change effectively.

While there are some local churches that will be lost if we don't change, there's more at stake than that. There's a generation that won't know the power of people committed to self-sacrifice and transforming both themselves and the wider community through the Gospel. A generation that may never see the waters part because no one stood at the edge of the Red Sea and begged God to do something. A generation that will be lost because the previous generation didn't have the courage to break away from the slow death that comes with the embrace of the status quo.

🎬 **To hear more from Carey about "What's at Stake?" go to LeadingChangeWithoutLosingIt.com.**

FOUR THINGS THAT HAPPEN TO DREAMS (AND DREAMERS)

When attempts at change fail, both dreams and dreamers suffer. Most often, one of four things happens when a dream encounters resistance and opposition:

1. **Your dream dies.** And with it, so does something inside you. Your passion, vision, imagination, and hope become fainter with each passing day.

2. **You settle for incremental change.** Because you couldn't get the results you yearned for, you settle. You end up compromising to a level that, over time, kills passion and vision. Things aren't transformed nearly as much as they could be or should be. You aren't dreaming anymore; you're settling. It's hard to fuel passion when you settle.

3. **You leave.** You may choose to leave the organization, quitting out of frustration and disillusionment, and look for another venue with better prospects. You may have little choice in the matter; maybe they ask you to go. And so you start again, only to realize there is a pattern here. What was difficult to implement last time is still difficult—sometimes more difficult—to bring about at your next ministry. Or (and this happens thousands of times each year) you give up on ministry altogether and go work at something entirely different. Whatever call there might have been will have to go unrealized. Poorly engineered change killed it. Or you. Or both.

4. **You learn how to lead change successfully.** This route seems mysterious. But there are leaders who have managed to bring about change, even transformation, despite opposition. They see their dreams realized.

That's what this book is about. While there is no guarantee that a strategy can bring about effective change
every time, there is a way to usher in change that can
increase the likelihood of success. We'll explore that
path in THREE BOOKS* (beginning with how to lead amidst
opposition, the focus of this book) largely because if
you're engineering change of any kind, that's exactly
what you're facing right now.

While no one can promise that you will successfully negotiate
all the change you are attempting to orchestrate, I can promise
you leaders do manage to navigate change. It is possible to
see your dream realized. You don't necessarily have to die to
your hopes, settle, or leave.

There's a dynamic to change. And it can be learned. If change
is as much about strategy as it is about pure inspiration, then
it's possible that all of us could become better navigators of
change no matter where we serve or what position we might
hold.

FIVE STRATEGIES FOR LEADING CHANGE WITHOUT LOSING IT

So, before you lose your mind, your dream, or your job, how
exactly *do* you lead people through change? To put it simply
(hint: this is the main idea of this book): **People who lead
change without losing it develop strategies that lead to the
right focus on the right things at the right moment.**

The right strategy is everything. So much of life is strategic. If
you want to become a faster cyclist, trying harder isn't always
effective. Sometimes big improvements happen from seeming-

ly small things like proper hydration, nutrition, seat height, seat position (forward or back), and even placement of your hands on the handlebars for different segments of the ride. Your strategy impacts your success almost more than your heart does. Sometimes we forget this in ministry.

Good strategies for change are about focusing on the right people in the right moments. Because many of us in ministry have pastoral hearts, it's difficult for us not to focus on everyone. After all, doesn't everyone matter to God?

But leaders who lead change effectively develop the right focus on the right things at the right moment. In this book, we want to show you how to do that. We'll look at five strategies that can help guide you through any organizational change you are undertaking:

1. **Do the math.** *Calculate who is actually opposed.* People who oppose things tend to get loud. This strategy will show you that, while it's easy to think otherwise, the loudest voices are not always the most important voices.

2. **Choose your focus.** *Decide whether you will focus on who you want to reach or who you want to keep.* As a leader, it's difficult to know who to focus on. But leaders who successfully navigate change realize that focusing on the complaints make you lose focus on the plan.

3. **Find a filter.** *Develop the questions that will shape your future.* Knowing you need to focus on the right people is one thing, but when you've got a cacophony of voices around you, how do you know which people it's most critical to hear? That's why finding a filter matters so much. Without a filter, everything sounds compelling.

4. **Attack problems, not people.** *Help people see you are for them even if you are not for their ideas.* Conflict can get heated. And you can sincerely disagree with people. But how do you do that without hurting people? We'll explore how turning to God can keep you from turning on "them."

5. **Don't quit.** *Persevere until your critical breakthrough.* It's hard to see change through to the end, but so worth it. We'll look at how to hang on when you feel like giving up. It's critical to persevere, because people who quit can often forfeit their place in the story God's writing.

While there are certainly other strategies at play, I have personally found that by focusing on these five, change becomes easier to navigate. My hope is that they help you in the same way they've helped me and other leaders.

While this book is about what these strategies will do, there are a few things these ideas *won't* do. They won't, for example, tell you how to develop a vision, nor will they tell you what the content of your vision should be. This book assumes that you have prayerfully worked that out. There are many resources designed to help you develop a vision. If your vision is simply misguided, I'm not sure any set of principles will save the day.

These strategies also assume that the vision you have is wise, sound, God-honoring, and that, for these reasons, it's a change people will ultimately embrace. Please stop and re-read that last sentence. It's critical. Sometimes people think they are speaking for God and steamroll others who disagree with them. Humility is always the companion of a great vision, and if your vision lacks that, you're missing a fundamental and necessary ingredient in a God-given vision. These strategies only work if the leader has a God-given vision embraced by a wider team and implemented with a quiet but confident humility.

The final thing these strategies will not do is eliminate pain. Unfortunately, pain is a necessary part of change leadership, even if you have an incredibly faithful and ultimately effective God-given vision.

YOU'VE GOT A FRIEND IN MOSES

The good news for those of us who have dreams of a better future is that you are not alone. If you were to study the issue of change through the lens of Scripture, you would quickly discover almost every biblical "hero" is a hero in large measure because he or she led people through complex change at critical moments. We can glean insights from these people, and at a minimum, perhaps empathize with them in a way that only fellow travelers can.

We could flip through many biblical accounts to find similar patterns of leading change in the face of opposition (Jesus, Timothy, David, the major and minor prophets, Joseph, and so many more); however, we'll center this book around the story of Moses delivering the Israelites out of slavery. Why that one? In part, because it is an epic struggle that ranks among the greatest in Scripture. But I want to turn to it for another reason: while the story is largely chronicled in Exodus and Deuteronomy, we have a gripping, personal, and powerful additional account in Numbers.

As I've led change in the context of the two ministries I've served in over the years, three particular chapters in Numbers (11, 12, and 14) have become constant companions. At times

I could hardly believe what I was reading. They seem like a behind-the-scenes documentary that takes the reader into the mind, heart, and struggle of Moses, the people, and even God.

In these passages, emotions are laid bare. These accounts are so candid that many times I just shook my head and said, "I can't believe this is actually in the Bible." These chapters have offered comfort, encouragement, and hope for me season after season. Like an older, wiser friend who has "been there," these passages have helped me understand that whatever we struggle with as navigators of change today, we have incredible company throughout history. God knows and understands. So did Moses.

While Moses didn't follow "five strategies" or "seven simple steps" toward change, interestingly enough you can find reasonably strong parallels for the five strategies we discuss in this book in those passages from Numbers. As we examine them, I hope they'll encourage and assist you in the ways they've helped me.

So before you start feeling alone, remember you are not. You are in great company. In fact, I challenge you to find a single leader in Scripture who did not encounter opposition to a meaningful change. I doubt you'll be able to. Why? Because they don't exist.

So, let's move on to the first strategy for leading change.

STRATEGY
DO THE MATH

DO THE MATH

Calculate who is actually opposed.

MOSES, UNCUT

You ever read a local church history book? You know, the kind that celebrates a 50th or 100th anniversary? I didn't think so. Why would you? They're a bit dull. And a bit untrue.

I mean they're true in the sense that they describe who chaired the board of elders in 1946, that the extension to the kitchen happened in 1958, and that the school bus ministry reached 311 children in the summer of 1974.

But congregational histories miss the fights. They don't talk about how 18 people stormed out of the church for good because the kitchen expansion project was outrageously expensive and doctrinally unsound. Or how the church bus driver got fired in 1975 for playing The Rolling Stones on the stereo. Nor do they mention the night the youth group hijacked the school bus and went off-roading. Local church histories typically miss the good stuff.

Not so with the Bible. At times, it's downright surprising in its detail. Sometimes it's like being the first to arrive at a dinner party only to walk in and find your hosts screaming at each other full volume in the kitchen.

Which is one reason I've become so grateful for Scripture. It tells the truth in gritty detail. For example, the account of Moses and the Israelites being freed from slavery, crossing the desert, and entering the Promised Land reads less like Charlton Heston and more like *The Dark Knight*.

The journey was peppered with conflict, accusation, desperation, and gut-honest emotion. Despite the fact that the former slaves were free and heading to a new home in the single greatest act of liberation on the front side of Easter, the people weren't happy.

> The foreign rabble who were traveling with the Israelites began to crave the good things of Egypt. And the people of Israel also began to complain. "Oh, for some meat!" they exclaimed. "We remember the fish we used to eat for free in Egypt. And we had all the cucumbers, melons, leeks, onions, and garlic we wanted. But now our appetites are gone. All we ever see is this manna!" (Numbers 11:4-6, NLT)

All they were seeing were the good things of the past (and even those through rose-colored glasses), conveniently overlooking the bad. What about the crushing toil of slave labor, the beatings and other physical cruelties, the heartless murder of their babies? Some things may have been good in Egypt, but they certainly weren't "free." They were paid for with every drop of blood and sweat of the people. The discomfort of the desert, combined with the unease of not knowing what the future held, appeared to divert the Israelites' attention. Instead of longing for the past, they would've been better off looking forward to the good things God had planned for their future.

Dissatisfaction with their new lives in the wilderness was not an occasional occurrence. A read through Scripture shows that Moses faced steady opposition to his leadership. Here's the rest of the scene that paints a portrait of what was quickly becoming the new normal in the desert:

> Moses heard all the families standing in the doorways of their tents whining, and the Lord became extremely angry. Moses was also very aggravated. (Numbers 11:10, NLT)

That must have been quite the day. The people were whining. Moses was frustrated. And God was angry. Talk about no safe place to hide.

Ever been there?

Not one of us who is trying to lead change in the face of opposition is the first person to meet resistance. Sometimes we try to convince ourselves—or even God—that we're the only ones who have it this tough. But that's not true, not even close. God understands. And when you join the company of those who lead change, you sign up for conflict. Ironically, pursuing a God-given vision doesn't mean you'll be exempt from opposition. Just the opposite: it almost guarantees you'll get some.

So when opposition arises, two questions emerge:

1. **How much actual opposition *is* there?**

2. **Of all the voices you hear, which ones should guide you?**

One of the best ways to address those questions is to simply do the math. In this book we'll explore five strategies for leading effective change but, while each is critical, it's important that you grasp this first strategy. Not because it is more important than the others, but because there is so much riding on it and it's the one leaders most easily miss. There is so much at stake in this. If you don't learn how to "do the math of opposition" as a leader, you'll let your emotions—not the math—guide your hearing. And leaders who do that often end up back in Egypt.

IT'S JUST MATH

So much of life is just math. Weight loss, for example, is math. Burn more calories than you eat, and you will lose weight. Becoming financially healthy is just simple math. Spend less than you make and you'll be financially sound. I'm writing this chapter 35,000 feet in the air. Although I like flying, I'm trusting that a lot of great math has gone into both the construction and operation of this plane. Math is everywhere. And It's even helpful in the church while attempting to lead change.

While I was never an astute math student (pi is something you eat, not something you factor in, or whatever), this math is so simple anyone can do it. When you understand how helpful the math is when engineering change, my guess is you'll never navigate another change without it. I believe it will give you a perspective that will help you keep your dream alive.

To keep it interesting, let's not start the discussion with ministry. Let's talk about a change we've all seen and even participated in to one extent or another.

One Phone. Four Kinds of People.

When you try to introduce change in virtually any arena, you get a variety of responses. They range from "enthusiastic embrace" to "deep resistance." What's notable is that people's responses are, for the most part, predictable. In fact, experts promote various accounts of how the population breaks down in response to ADAPTATION TO CHANGE[2]. What follows here is a slightly adapted model of how people respond to change. For fun, let's look at these trends through the lens of how four people-groups respond to something like the introduction of the latest smartphone:

1. **Early Adopters.** These are the people who enthusiastically embrace and adopt change. They're the ones who either line up for days to get the latest phone the moment it's released or pre-order it seconds after it's available online. They love change. They thrill at being first. In many areas of life, they are leaders. Not all leaders are Early Adopters, but most Early Adopters are leaders, and they line up around the block for new things with smiles on their faces.

2. **Early Majority.** The Early Majority are similar to their Early Adopter friends, just one time zone behind. They like change. They're enthusiastic about progress. But they'll get the phone when it's back in stock. Sure, they may check inventory levels from time to time, but they won't go camping to get it. Still, they'll have the latest phone before many of their friends do. And they'll love its features.

3. **Quiet Majority.** These people like phones, but they think about the hassle of changing their cell phone plans and the upgrade costs. They like technology and

usually pick up something new at some point. But for
right now, the phone they have is fine. Eventually, the
Quiet Majority will carry the phone in question just like the
Early Adopters and Early Majority, but it might be because
they unwrap it at Christmas. They're not really opposed.
They're just not first, and sometimes not second. They're
waiting to see where the culture goes and ultimately,
they'll follow it.

4. **Opponents.** This group has a variety of viewpoints
   among its members, but what unites them is their opposition to change. The Opponents I'm referring to in
   this book are rarely people with a future-oriented sense
   of vision or purpose. When it comes to phones, you've
   seen the type: Some can't believe another phone is
   being released when nothing is wrong with the current
   models. They want the madness to stop. Also in this
   group are people who are still getting used to their land-
   lines and fax machines. In fact, there are a few who still
   ride horses to deliver messages. Usually, these people
   oppose all things new. They don't like that shirt you're
   wearing either, now that you mention it.

Recognize the pattern? Of course you do. You are in one of
those groups (although you're probably an Early Adopter or
Early Majority if you're reading this book). But you don't have to
look far to find people you know in each category. Most significantly, all four groups attend your church.

So what do you do about the four groups? The answer is
"math."

To keep things simple, let's assume you are leading 100 people through some kind of significant change. While the percentage of the population within each group is debatable, and while it might change depending on the context, the following percentages are generally true in most cases:

Whether the percentage varies a little or a lot in your context is less important than watching what happens when these groups begin to speak into any change you propose. And I suspect I know where you are going. You are thinking, "There's no way only 10% of the people in my church are opposed to change. It's more like 30%, or 50%, or more." If that's what you're thinking, just hang on.

LOUD ≠ LARGE AND VOLUME ≠ VELOCITY

The loudest people affected by a proposed change are those who are most opposed. The more opposed people are, the louder they tend to become. The problem arises because the noise of Opponents to any change will make you a bad mathematician.

You will confuse loud with large. And you will confuse volume with velocity. You will begin to believe that because Opponents are loud, they are many, and because they have volume, they have momentum.

Those are the two traps almost every leader falls into at some point. We simply assume loud means large, and that volume signals velocity.

But loud does not equal large. And volume does not equal velocity. Just because a voice is loud doesn't mean you should listen to it most.

Think through it: the kind of people who oppose things as a matter of course often don't have an alternative vision. In fact, they are rarely going anywhere. Sometimes they're just angry. If they want anything, it's either the status quo or, like the Israelites, a one-way ticket back to Egypt.

That's because Opponents generally don't possess a vision for the future, only a vision for the past which—if you think about it—is an impossible vision. It's actually impossible to move to what was; you can only move to what will be. Often, Opponents are stuck, and if they gain too much influence, your organization might also end up stuck with them.

Imagine if Moses had listened to the Opponents. Imagine if he had decided to give in and do what the Opponents wanted. A nation's future hung in the balance. God, I'm sure, would have found a way to work around that, but both Moses and the people would have been miserable once they were back in Egypt. The only winner in the story might have been Pharaoh.

So who are the compelling voices to listen to? Well, consider for a moment what you might be hearing (or missing) from the Early Adopters and the Early Majority. The well-thought-out change they support is going somewhere. A progressive vision of the future has a trajectory of hope. Opposition doesn't. Although it's loud, it's seldom helpful.

EASY AS 1-2-3

So let's do a little more math. The following diagram shows some of the dynamics of the four groups as they encounter a proposal for change:

The trends in this graph represent what usually happens in the face of change.

Although percentages will vary slightly, the number of people opposed to wise and worthwhile change is generally a small minority, which for our purposes we've set at 10%. The reason it never feels like just 10% is because Opponents are loud. But remember: leading change through opposition distorts reality. It distorts our perception as leaders so badly that we usually get our math deeply wrong. If you want to avoid a common mistake leaders make, remember this: never confuse loud with large. Don't let pushback distort your perspective.

One of the reasons it's so easy to confuse loud with large is because people who are opposed to change claim to speak for more than just themselves. They say "everyone" is upset, "so many people" are angry, and "lots of people" feel the same way they do. Naturally, you don't fall for the "everyone" language, but deep down you think a majority could be opposed to the change. If you've never done the math and realized that Opponents typically constitute a small percentage of the population, it's easy to assume that the 10% is 30% or even 70% of the congregation. Loud just got large in your mind, even though that might be the furthest thing from the truth.

LOUD IS ... MEMORABLE

I don't want to let this thought go because it's so easy to lose the math in the emotion. Five years ago, we were navigating significant change. I was getting ready to leave my current denomination, which also meant leaving the building we had constructed five years earlier to start all over again. In the midst of that, I had a moment that reminded me of how powerful loud can be. We had three morning services and my office was just off the main hallway of our building. I had slipped into my office to collect a few things between services when a woman I'll call Beth knocked on my door.

She was visibly angry, but I wasn't ready for what came next. She walked in, leaned over the desk toward me, and started to tell me how angry she was about my leaving. Only she wasn't speaking. She was screaming. At the top of her lungs. About three feet away from me.

I didn't know what to do. I'm certainly not saying I was right and she was wrong, but I am saying her voice was loud. I think I was in shock. I just stood, speechless, motionless, and listened. I had no idea what to say. It was like all my senses went numb. At the end of the five-minute tirade, I mumbled something about being sorry she felt that way. She left. I was shell-shocked. Then it occurred to me that I had to go and somehow lead worship.

How do you *not* listen to a voice that loud? There were maybe 800 other people in the building that morning. But Beth's voice is the only voice I remember from that day.

Which is why the math is so critical. Loud may be memorable, but loud does not equal large, and volume does not equal velocity. There actually are other (helpful) voices. They're just quieter.

LISTEN ... REALLY LISTEN

For example, the Early Majority and Quiet Majority aren't saying much, if anything, at this point. For the most part they're quietly supportive or neutral. And the Early Adopters are on board, but they're not as loud as the Opponents.

Which means—don't miss this—that even on the day when someone is screaming at you in your office, as much as 90%

of your organization is not directly opposed to the direction you and your team are taking.

Leaders who listen carefully will also realize the Early Adopters have been saying a few things as well; it's just usually more civil and easier to miss. Here's what you'll hear from them when you take the time to listen:

"I'm excited about the change."

"I've been waiting for this for a long time."

"Way to go!"

"This is the direction we need to head in. This is good."

As you can see, it's so critical for you as a leader to be intentional about which voices guide your hearing. Here's why:

When you listen to the loudest voices, you miss the most important voices.

In the midst of the crisis, you need to let the math, not your emotions, guide your hearing.

To hear more from Carey about "Early Adopters," go to LeadingChangeWithoutLosingIt.com.

DON'T TRUST YOUR INBOX

The other perception that confuses the situation for leaders is the worry that the number of Opponents is growing. As the 10% organize and take up a few rows in a meeting, you begin to mistake their increasing volume with increasing velocity, or momentum. Because you keep hearing about "everyone" and "lots of people" and "the whole group," you imagine this group gathering steam and heading somewhere. If you could trust your inbox, you would swear that's what's happening. Because the volume's up, you assume an increase in velocity as well. Now while opposition might grow for a certain season, it's almost never as large as it seems. (In fact, in Strategies 3 and 4, we'll look at how to mitigate opposition and how to attempt to grow the support base for change.)

But as the following diagram illustrates, the momentum around change is likely moving in the right direction, even when it might feel like it's not. Remember that Opponents for the most part are stuck, and the Early Adopters and the Early Majority are or will be the people who have velocity because they're embracing a vision that is heading places. If your vision is going somewhere good, it has a momentum of its own that will become clearer with the passage of time, provided you don't cave to the pressure to go back to Egypt.

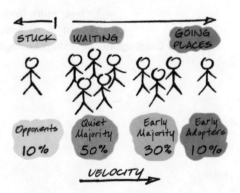

So, in the midst of your most emotional and confusing days, ask yourself a couple of key questions:

1. Am I confusing loud with large?

2. Am I confusing volume with velocity?

BUT HOW DO I SLEEP AT NIGHT?

So navigating change at this level doesn't exactly feel like a vacation, does it? But there is something that can help you sleep better at night. And no, it's not a pill. It's a perspective.

Before we move any further, let's recap what we've covered so far:

10% are opposed and loud (Opponents)

10% are audibly enthusiastic (Early Adopters)

30% are inaudibly supportive (Early Majority)

50% are quietly neutral to hopeful (Quiet Majority)

You can see where this is going, right? Forty percent of the organization (Early Adopters and Early Majority) are probably already on board. Another 50% is quietly supportive to neutral. Only 10% are opposed.

So think this through. Even though the Opponents have volume and claim to have velocity (but don't), they represent about a tenth of your organization. That's it. Did you hear that? Ninety percent either will be or are already in favor of change. I realize it doesn't feel like that. I understand it doesn't sound like that.

But that doesn't mean it isn't true.

So if you were going to listen only to the Opponents, here's what you would be doing as a leader: *you would be sacrificing the interests and desires of 90% of your people for the sake of 10%.*

Is that actually what you want to do? Do you really want the preferences of 10% to control the destiny of the other 90%?

I understand that you're worried the 10% will leave. You're also worried that the 10% in your case is not 10% but 30%, or 40%. I doubt it, but let's say it was. *Will you sacrifice the remaining 60% for the sake of 40%, or the remaining 70% for the sake of 30%?*

If you're still uncomfortable, and the math isn't yet compelling enough, start thinking bigger. Think outside the walls of your organization. If your mission has anything to do with reaching people in your community, this next sequence is critical.

Let's assume the 100 people you are trying to lead through change live in a wider community of 10,000. Allowing the 10% of your organization who are opposed to change to win the day would mean you decide not to reach 99.999% of your community because .001% of your community got loud in their opposition.

Let that sink in: *if you were to give in to that pressure from them, you would be letting 10 people jeopardize the future of 9,990.* Even if your opposition is greater—say 50% of your group is opposed to change—that means you would be allow-ing 50 people to decide that your church will never reach 9,950 of its neighbors.

I didn't think you would want to do that.

Before you decide you can't lead with opposition at 50%, let me tell you about how our ministry began at the original three churches back in my student days. I was fresh out of law and had begun seminary, struggling with whether God was actually calling me to ministry. As my wife and I prayed through the whole issue of calling, we began to look at the possibility of taking what is called a "student charge." A student charge in that denomination is a cluster of two or three churches that share a pastor—a student pastor—because they can't afford a full-time ordained minister. (It would be better to pretend it was more theological than that, but it wasn't. And when you're a student, you're just grateful for the chance to be in a church.)

We found three churches an hour north of Toronto who were looking for a student. I called; they interviewed me and invited me to preach. But they also wanted a choice of pastors. My classmate and good friend Charles had submitted his candidacy for the position as well. Neither of us realized until later that we were both candidates for the same job.

Charles was invited to preach one weekend and I was invited to speak the next. If you've ever heard or met my friend Charles, you'll realize he's incredible—a truly gifted communicator and a man after God's own heart. I spoke at the churches the week after Charles preached and gave it my best shot. We both interviewed on separate nights with the elders, and then they voted.

On the night of the vote I got a call indicating I was THEIR CHOICE[3]. I had "won," I was told, by one vote. Not really thinking it through but believing God was in it, I accepted. We moved our family from Toronto and started ministry there.

Now I realize you're a little ahead of me in the story, but truthfully it was only on my first Sunday as their pastor as I stood up to preach that it dawned on me that 50% of the people in our congregation didn't want me as their pastor. I know. Not exactly Mensa level processing on my part.

But it is proof it's possible to lead change even when almost half the congregation doesn't want you as their pastor. Within five years we had transitioned our style of worship, sold all three buildings, and amalgamated the three congregations into one, growing 300% in the process.

That said, let's dial the opposition back to the more typical 1 in 10 who oppose. By paying more attention to the 10%, you can ruin the future of almost 10,000 people—just because of the noise 10 people make. Who would want to be responsible for that? That simple math (of not being willing to sacrifice the interests of 99% for the sake of 1%) helped me sleep at night. It made me realize we were heading somewhere. Somewhere good.

BETTER MATH MAKES FOR BETTER LEADERS

That's the math of opposition. Not only do numbers not lie, but numbers can lead you closer to the truth of what's really going on and what actually "could be and should be" for your organization, for your community, and for you. Just because voices are loud doesn't mean they are the only or most important voices to listen to. If you're not careful, you'll miss the voice of the future as you listen to the voice of the past. There are always people who want to go back to Egypt or anywhere but where change leads them.

As you lead through opposition, make sure you stop to do some math. Calculate who is actually opposed. If you let the math, not your emotions, direct your decisions, you will become a more effective leader.

📽 **For a Bonus Video, go to LeadingChangeWithoutLosingIt.com and click on "Quick Tip: Doing the Math."**

2

STRATEGY

CHOOSE
YOUR FOCUS

STRATEGY 2

CHOOSE YOUR FOCUS

Decide whether you will focus on who you want to reach or who you want to keep.

A LITTLE UNFOCUSED

Although I've never been officially diagnosed, I suspect I'm a little ADD. I have trouble staying focused, especially in meetings. I can drift off and completely miss the conversation or even blurt out random things I just happened to be thinking about, which may or may not have much to do with the topic at hand.

Technology hasn't made it any easier for those of us who are easily distracted. With multiple inboxes, push notifications, and Tweets that make my phone chirp, ting, and produce other intriguing noises, I'll often jump to something else before I get what I'm working on completed. When my assistant was away a few years ago, I decided to book my own flight for some meetings in Atlanta, despite the fact that there were many things vying for my attention that week. I got a good rate on the tickets; however, I booked the flight backward. Instead of flying from Toronto to Atlanta and back, I booked the tickets for Atlanta to Toronto and back. Not very helpful when you live in Toronto. Fortunately, Sarah came back from vacation and solved quite a few problems I had created in her absence.

Focus is a big issue for leaders, and distraction can cause more than a little inconvenience. The only way I know how to

solve focus issues in ministry (and life) is to discipline myself.
Really discipline myself.

Leading change can be an incredible test of focus. How, for
example, can you *not* focus on who's loudest when you're
navigating change? Doing the math (see Strategy 1) definitely
helps, but you'll need more than that. You'll need to choose
your focus. Because focus, like so many things in life, is a
choice.

AN UNBELIEVABLE FOCUS

Moses was in a perfect position to lose focus. If he had chosen
to pay attention only to what was going on around him, it would
have been almost impossible for him to keep going.

In one passage I find particularly astonishing, Moses seems
about the only one left (with the exception of Joshua and
Caleb) who believed in the vision for change. When the spies
returned from exploring the Promised Land and made their
report (Numbers 13), the whole community began to weep
aloud. They cried all night, agitating each other so much that,
by morning, there was wide-scale, full-blown rebellion. They
turned on Moses and his brother Aaron, making it personal:
"Let's choose a new leader and go back to Egypt!" (Numbers 14:4, NLT). Not a lot of gratitude for the sacrifices Moses
had made on their behalf.

As the situation deteriorated, God intervened. He said to
Moses:

> **"How long will these people treat me with contempt?
> Will they never believe me, even after all the miracu-**

> lous signs I have done among them? I will disown
> them and destroy them with a plague. Then I will
> make you into a nation greater and mightier than
> they are!" (Numbers 14:11-12, NLT)

Clearly God had had it. What's not so clear, perhaps, was
God's intent. Was He making Moses a bona fide offer? "I'll ex-
tinguish all these people who are making your life miserable. In
fact, I'll establish you as the new Abraham and make you into
a nation greater and stronger than these people ever were."
(What leader hasn't thought about that, if even for a second, by
the way? For opposition to just miraculously evaporate in moments seems like an attractive option.)

Now this is a tricky passage to navigate. Was God expressing
His righteous anger, using the opportunity to teach Moses (and
thereby the people) how disastrous the sin of distrust can be?
Was He testing Moses' heart? Was He using the opportunity to
strengthen Moses for the long haul ahead of him?

Whatever God's purpose, here's how Moses responded:

> "What will the Egyptians think when they hear about
> it?" he asked the Lord. "They know full well the pow-
> er you displayed in rescuing your people from Egypt.
> Now if you destroy them, the Egyptians will send
> a report to the inhabitants of this land, who have
> already heard that you live among your people. They
> know, Lord, that you have appeared to your people
> face to face and that your pillar of cloud hovers over
> them. They know that you go before them in the pil-
> lar of cloud by day and the pillar of fire by night. Now
> if you slaughter all these people with a

single blow, the nations that have heard of your fame will say, "The Lord was not able to bring them into the land he swore to give them, so he killed them in the wilderness." (Numbers 14:13-16, NLT)

I find Moses' response astonishing. I'm not sure many leaders would have responded the same way. I'm not sure I would have. Moses kept his focus on fulfilling the original plan, which is even more amazing when you consider that the original vision wasn't even his idea. Remember? He was tending sheep and living a happy life in obscurity when God interrupted him with a burden for an enslaved people, a people He loved.

Moses' focus was set: it wasn't on himself, and it wasn't on the perceived emotional needs and wants of "insiders" (they changed hourly, after all). It could only be on one thing: doing what God had called him to do in the first place. Because the exile was so "public" (600,000+ slaves who drive the economic engine of a global superpower don't disappear without notice), the eyes of every nation were on Israel. Outsiders were watching, and Moses was concerned about their perception of God:

> "Please, Lord, prove that your power is as great as you have claimed." (Numbers 14:17, NLT)

Moses was far more concerned about how outsiders would be impacted than he was about what insiders wanted. His focus was unshakeable. He knew that …

When you focus on complaints, you lose sight of the plan.

And because of his decision to focus on the plan, the story unfolded differently. In that is a lesson for us.

Despite the fact that Moses wasn't a perfect leader (he did deal with anger and frustration unwisely at times), he knew God is very concerned about outsiders, and he saw it as his responsibility to maintain that focus no matter what. He chose to focus on what few others were seeing in the moment. And that's how focus works. Focus is always a choice. One of the most important questions you'll ever answer as a leader is this: Will you focus on the people you want to reach, or the people you want to keep?

Now of course, the church must do both: reach the unbeliever *and* disciple the insider. This is not about serving one to the exclusion of the other. But it's easy to forget about people not in the room because we only hear the people who are in the room. (More on that later.) In the midst of the conflict associated with change, your focus will be tested again and again. This is true of churches who are navigating their first big push toward change in years, but it's also true of churches that have had a successful track record of change, like church plants and churches that are experiencing current success. Just because you're reaching unchurched people today is no guarantee you will reach them tomorrow. And because the voices opposing further change are loud, it's too easy for church leaders to rest on current successes and declare victory too soon. Leaders need to keep their focus on who they want to reach, not just who they want to keep, in every season.

 To hear more about "Focus,"
go to LeadingChangeWithoutLosingIt.com.

When I first heard this idea—that of focusing on who you want to reach, not who you want to keep, from **ANDY STANLEY, REGGIE JOINER, AND LANE JONES**[4]—it made a profound impact on me. Most church leaders who attempt to transition their church pay close attention to not losing the people they have. I've felt that tug inside me too. But the pull to keep insiders can compete with the push to reach outsiders. And reaching outsiders is something that speaks to many of us. I don't know any church leaders who freely say they have no interest in reaching outsiders—last time I checked, most church leaders with a pulse agreed that people matter to God and should matter to us. Even more than that, the core motivation for much of the desired change in the 21st century church springs from our ineffectiveness at connecting with outsiders.

The problem, then, lies not in what we say we want or feel we need. It lies in what we do with our focus.

Three years into my work as a senior pastor, I had a moment that forever sealed a focus on outsiders into my heart. One morning as I was preaching what was for all intents and purposes a regular Sunday message, I had a searing sense (call it the Spirit of God) that God was more interested in the people outside the walls of our church than He was in the people inside the walls. Fourteen years later, I can still vividly recall the view I had from the pulpit that day ... this unnaturally keen sense that beyond the century-old stained glass were people Christ was longing to be in relationship with, and that we were called to do something about that. Dozens of times when I've been discouraged, that sense of "call" has kept me committed to what I believe is the most pressing mission the church has.

The question is, how do you keep that focus in the emotional crucible of change?

SO ... HOW DO YOU STAY FOCUSED?

It would be great if there were some practical game plan for keeping focused on outsiders: "Do these three simple things and you will never lose focus." But focus isn't that simple. This is as much about your heart and self-discipline as anything.

Sometimes when something as theoretical as "focus" is at issue, the best way I stay on track is to remind myself of the "why" behind the "what." For example, in order to stay in reasonable shape, I remind myself God controls the length of my life, but my diet and exercise choices have a direct impact on the quality of the life He gives me. That helps me a lot.

Similarly, when it comes to focusing on who you want to reach, not who you want to keep, the why behind the what helps keep my focus sharper.

So let's review some basics we all know. First, there is a compelling reason God wants us to reach outsiders: He sacrificed His Son out of love for the world. The mission of the early church reflected this. The thrust of Scripture and the movement of the Gospel is outward. If the twelve disciples had focused on who they were going to keep rather than who they were going to reach, they might have quit after losing Judas or spent the next decade trying to get Thomas to quit doubting and Peter to stop being so impulsive. We stand in a long line of leaders who have been entrusted with a Gospel whose central movement is outward.

Biblical reasons should be enough, for sure, but there are also practical reasons to keep focused on outsiders. I have come to believe that leaders who focus on who they want to reach have less quit in them, and discover a well of deeper inspiration, more powerful motivation, and greater hope. As a result, I believe leaders who keep a focus on outsiders are more resilient than leaders who don't. When you strive toward a goal that is bigger than yourself, bigger than your congregation, and bigger than your own wants and needs, you discover a drive you didn't know you had.

For many of the same reasons, focusing on who you want to reach creates a far more compelling storyline for your vision. And outward-focused vision is simply more compelling than a vision that is self-focused or rooted in the status quo. People rally around visions that are about others. Despite our self-centeredness, there is something deep inside each of us that wants to make our lives about something bigger than ourselves. Great leaders call that out of us and motivate us around that. If you want to create a vision that inspires others, don't make it about yourself or simply the needs of your organization.

WHY IS FOCUSING ON WHO YOU WANT TO REACH SO DIFFICULT?

It's easy to focus on people you want to keep. It takes much more resolve to focus on those you want to reach.

Here's why. You have to focus on people you haven't even met. It's easier and more natural to focus on people whose stories you know, who are paying your bills, and who are going to vote in the next congregational meeting. It's much more difficult and requires significantly more intentionality to focus on people who are not yet a part of your church. Unchurched people never fill up your inboxes with messages telling you they would come if you changed this one thing. They don't show up to meetings with petitions begging you to be more relevant. They've never taken you out for lunch to explain how "everyone" they know would come to your church if you did family ministry better. They don't call saying they'd love to have you share the Gospel while feeding them, clothing them, or visiting them. They don't send emails saying, "Please come help the kids who live in our subsidized housing unit."

Most of the people in the community you are trying to reach are unaware of or indifferent to the fact that you exist. As a leader, it's your responsibility to keep them front of mind. (One of the best ways of doing that, by the way, is to make sure you have lots of unchurched friends in your social circle that you pray for regularly.)

BUT WHAT IF WE LOSE PEOPLE?

The number one question people ask me when I talk about change is this: What if we lose people? The truth is, our church lost people in all the transition. You probably will too. There is no way I know to engineer significant change and keep everyone you've currently got. People tend to like things the way they are. In fact, everyone in your church likes your church the way it is; otherwise, they wouldn't be there. It's just that the rest of your community may not. Otherwise, they might be there.

If you change, some who like the status quo more than they like change may leave.

How many? Enough. Some of the 10% opposed to change will go. Maybe less, maybe more. And if you make radical changes, you might lose 10% again next year. There may be cumulative losses because the kind of community you're forming will start looking radically different from others. But while the losses may be cumulative, the gains are potentially exponential.

In our case, there were only two seasons in 15 years when we stopped growing: when we eliminated hymns entirely from our service, and when we left a nearly paid-for building to start over again as a brand-new church. I'm not saying either of these is something congregations should do. We did them because we believed they would help us reach more people. Despite experiencing slight declines in the moment, we bounced back to reach even more people than we had prior to the change, people who were not going to church at all. I was reminded again and again that if you focus on complaints, you lose sight of the plan. We just couldn't afford to do that. So we shouldered some painful seasons.

Before you get too anxious (or too excited) about losing people, in the next chapter we'll develop some questions that will help you assess if you are losing the right people. (Yes, there may be people you should lose and there are people you should keep.) But until then, let's keep moving through this concept.

WHAT NOT TO FEAR

If there's one lingering reason church leaders are tempted to focus on who we want to keep instead of who we want to reach, I think it's fear. We're afraid that people will leave. We're afraid of who they'll take with them. We're afraid of what they'll say about us to others. We're worried about the financial impact of people leaving (even though they've likely checked out financially long before they've checked out of the building). We hate disappointing people. We don't like to be disliked. We don't want to be unpopular.

All of those are understandable reasons. But none of them is a *good* reason. Actually, they are selfish reasons. I've felt those fears as a leader. When you start to move through these fears, you grow as a person and as a leader. It's not fun growth (the fear is there because you think it's real), but it's powerful growth. A leader who learns that it's about far more than just how popular he or she is can actually develop a deeper humility in the process of developing a greater courage. Leaders like that are worth following. They have moved past leadership being about them and their insecurities. They are not leading for the sake of themselves. They are leading for the sake of Christ and others. And what those leaders discover, after some painful moments, is that there is freedom on the other side of their fear.

FEAR THIS

Okay, having just tried to convince you to move past your fears about change, I'm going to tell you now to do the opposite. There are some things I think a leader *should* fear. But they are very different from what we *naturally* fear.

So what should leaders fear? I think we should fear never reaching the people we're trying to reach. While you may have had some success in reaching some of the unchurched in your community (some of you, actually, have had incredible success), there are still more unreached than reached. Unless you bring about the change you're looking at, you are unlikely to reach them at all. So when you consider the 10 or 100 who might leave your church if you change, just pause to remember the almost 10,000 who aren't coming because, so far, you have failed to change. Maybe as leaders we need to start fearing that.

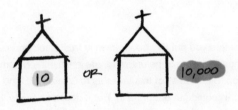

And here's another thing to fear. If you're worried about losing people, start worrying about losing the Early Adopters and Early Majority. They may not be as loud as the Opponents, but if you fail to change, at some point over the next year or two, you might lose many of them. They won't storm out angrily and they might not even tell you they're going. But if you continue to embrace the status quo for fear of the cost of change, many of them will slip away. That's true in traditional churches that are transitioning and in churches with a track record of past success. The greatest enemy of your future success is your current success. So deciding that you will continue to do what progress requires (even if your church is relatively new) will ensure you keep the right people in your organization. Listening to the quieter voices ensures you'll hear your organization's most important voices.

The Early Adopters and Early Majority really are waiting for you to do the right thing. They're waiting for you as a leader to lead. They want to be well led. They want to be inspired. Like you, they dream of a better tomorrow. And if they can't find it at your church, they'll look for it somewhere else.

So a question: Who would you rather lose? The Opponents, or the Early Adopters?

Exactly.

Now before you put this book down in frustration and claim this line of thinking to be unloving, unChristian, and unmerciful, hang on. Because all of this takes us to Strategy 3: Find a Filter. Sure, this could get out of hand. But it doesn't have to. In fact, working through Strategies 2 and 3 as you lose people might help you to become more biblically faithful than you realize.

▇ For a Bonus Video, go to LeadingChangeWithoutLosingIt.com and click on "Quick Tip: Choosing Your Focus."

3

STRATEGY

FIND A FILTER

STRATEGY 3

FIND A FILTER

Develop the questions that will shape your future.

YOU NEED A FILTER

We sometimes go camping as a family, even though I believe camping is inherently unChristian. (My belief: If God designed us with the intelligence to create buildings in which you can live comfortably all year long, filled with gadgets that use the electricity He created, isn't it just sinful to revert to a less developed way of life?) But I go because I love my family.

One of the issues when camping is having a reliable water supply. My wife and our friends always make sure we not only take clean water, but that we take filters that allow us to purify lake water and ground water so we can drink it. My friend Clyde (one of our good friends we camp with) has this large blue bag he hangs on a makeshift clothesline and fills with gallons of lake water that then drips through a filter to produce pure, clean, great-tasting water that's better than you'd find in most municipal water supplies. Plus it eliminates the parasites that would make even avid campers want to swear off the adventure for a season.

DO YOU HEAR VOICES?

As a leader, you need to find a filter. You have so many voices coming at you that you may not be sure whose voice to listen to. Since loud can easily be mistaken for large, and volume sometimes creates the illusion of velocity, the filter you develop is crucial.

In order to answer that need, let's start by reiterating some assumptions. Remember that we're working with the premise that you have a biblical vision for the change you want to bring about. We're also assuming that you have support from key leaders, and that this is a vision that resonates at a deep personal level with you. (I understand that will be tested at times, something we discuss in Strategy 5.) And let's presume you've done the math and decided what you're going to focus on.

Even if all that is true, none of that makes the voices go away. They keep coming at you. Sometimes relentlessly.

That's why it's so critical to drill down a level further. How do you develop a *good* filter? My friend Clyde had exactly the right filter with him. It was specially constructed to turn lake water into drinking water. If I had brought a coffee filter or a furnace filter from my home and used it, I'm quite sure some of us would have ended up in the emergency ward of the nearest hospital the next day. Even a conventional home water filter would have failed us.

Having the right filter helps you wrestle down a critical question every leader needs to answer: *How do I make sense of the voices raised in disagreement with the vision?* If you're a healthy leader, you're going to ask yourself some tough questions like:

- **What if the Opponents are right and those of us in favor of change are wrong?**
- **What if God is speaking through them and I'm missing it?**
- **What if my judgment is so off I can't tell what's right and what's wrong anymore?**

A good filter will guide you when you no longer know which way to turn. That's why it's so crucial you develop one.

So, exactly how do you do that? Early in my leadership, I realized I had to figure that out and figure it out fast.

EXPERIENCE IS A GOOD TEACHER

By the time I was three years into my leadership of the three small churches north of Toronto, the proposal for change we were looking at was radical, to say the least. In order to accommodate current and future growth and position ourselves for ministry to a fundamentally different culture that had emerged over the last 50 years, we would sell all three century-old buildings and create a new church on a new site with a new name. Essentially, we were asking people whose great-grandparents started the church to leave the past behind them, including their buildings. These were the buildings in which many of them had been baptized, in which they'd been married, and in which their own children had come to faith. All for an unknown future in a temporary location. It was brand-new territory for all of us.

Naturally, the proposal had its critics, both from within and without. Many people told me that what we were attempting was unprecedented (not entirely true: a church 50 miles away had done a similar thing with some success a decade earlier) and unlikely to work (that was probably more accurate). And, of course, the proposal evoked deep emotion among many in the congregation. How could we leave all this behind and start over again to reach people we didn't even know? They were great questions.

Congregational meetings are rarely fun, but we had a few over this issue that became more tense than usual. When you hear so many voices in opposition, what do you do? For sure, the loudest appeared to represent a large number of people. Even if they turned out to be a minority, what if those people were right? What if our leadership team were wrong? What if I were wrong in believing a move would be best?

I'm not exactly sure how it happened, but I do remember that it happened. I developed a filter. I sat down with our elders one night and said that we needed to come up with a method of sifting through the voices we were hearing. Informally at first, but very decidedly, we developed two questions through which we'd process every negative voice we heard:

1. **Is there a biblical argument in what the person is saying?**

2. **Is this person the kind of person we are going to build the future of the church on?**

There is nothing magic about these questions, nor am I suggesting they should be your questions. You might have better ones. I share them, and some thoughts behind them, for one reason: over the years, they have been exceptionally helpful and clarifying for me and for many on our team. Whenever there is opposition to change, they are the two questions I've learned to ask. I would encourage you to develop your own questions, because as we'll see in the balance of this chapter, the questions you ask determine the future you live.

QUESTION 1: IS THERE A BIBLICAL ARGUMENT?

If there is a biblical argument in someone's objection to a change, a leader has a duty to pay attention to it. God speaks through people. And if what people are saying is consistent with Scripture, it is very possible that you might be hearing from God through them. Even when you hear from people you don't necessarily like. At a minimum, you and I have to take their perspective seriously.

That said, in my experience it's actually not that often that Opponents of change talk about the Bible. Don't get me wrong. I'm not questioning their faith or even their motives. All I'm saying is that people who steadfastly oppose change often don't have a deeply biblical argument they're advancing.

They're more likely to fight about cultural preferences than they are about biblical principles. Discussions with Opponents are usually about one type of music over another, one model of family ministry over another, one building, budget, or staffing structure over another. People get passionate about their preferences and may even get entrenched in them, but at the end of the day little of it is really about being "right" or "wrong" theologically. Preferences, rather than principles, tend to be more front and center in these discussions, although people may fight just as hard about one as the other.

So what do you do with that as a leader? Treat it for what it is: a discussion about cultural preferences. You like sushi; I like steak. You don't have to be right for me to be wrong, and I don't have to be wrong for you to be right. We just have different preferences.

When we move beyond sushi and steak and into church strategy, the issues become more important. Even though there might not be a strong biblical argument in the discussion, some ways of being the church are actually more effective than others. For example, if a church is attempting to impact families, I believe it is going to have to invest in its children's ministry and student ministry. And, like it or not, our priorities tend to show up in our budgets (this is true personally and organizationally). So if proponents say reaching families is important, but the church invests 3% of its budget in family ministry, 15% in senior adult ministry, and 25% on sanctuary restoration, the budget just revealed the church's true priorities. Sure, people could start pulling Bible verses to support any viewpoint they wish, but in the end the budget (again, as the example) is about the church's cultural preferences and strategy. If a church wants to be ineffective with families, investing nothing in them is a great approach. There's not really a biblical argument at issue here; the discussion simply reveals a strategy anchored in preferences.

And if there's not a biblical argument in what an Opponent is saying, that leads us to the second question in this filter ...

QUESTION 2: ARE WE GOING TO BUILD THE FUTURE OF THE CHURCH ON THEM?

Is the person protesting the change the kind of person we're going to build the future of the church on? This one's tough, but it's incredibly helpful. This second question has helped steer our decisions countless times.

As difficult as it is to make judgment calls about people (see the next chapter for more on this), a leader needs to discern who the people will be that will help lead the organization into the future. That's not an easy task, and you should probably take time to pray about how you will personally approach this question. When navigating this issue, it's important always to keep the distinction between judgment and discernment clear. God's judgment is perfect, which is likely part of the reason Jesus told us not to judge. Somehow my personal judgment too often carries with it a sense of superiority. When I judge others it implies a sense that I am better or my understanding is better. It's imperative that leaders walk humbly through this principle. Leaders are not all knowing. And leaders can be wrong.

That's why I prefer to think of the process we need to engage in as discernment rather than judgment. Discernment simply seeks to understand.

In that spirit then, here are five questions designed to help you discern whether a person is indeed the kind of person you can build the future of the church on:

1. **Is their vision primarily based on the past or on the future?**

2. **Do they have a spirit of humility? Are they open or closed to the counsel of other people?**

3. **Who is following them, and is this the kind of group that you would want around your senior leadership table?**

4. **Are they focused on themselves or the people you are trying to reach?**

5. **Do they offer positive alternatives that will help build a better future than your current vision for change?**

I realize these questions can be painful to answer (and you never need to answer them out loud), but they can help you figure out how seriously to weigh the arguments of the Opponents to change. Often, unswerving opponents to change have few of the characteristics you will want in your future organization.

> **To hear more about "Developing Your Filter," go to LeadingChangeWithoutLosingIt.com.**

MOSES HAD A FILTER

So you might be asking, is this concept of "filter" even biblical? Great question. While your concordance won't take you to many "develop a biblical filter" passages and the relevant passages likely will never make any Hallmark card, I believe they exist. You have to do a bit of sleuthing to find them. But they're there.

Let's go back to Moses. While it's not exactly clear what Moses' filter was, it's evident he had one. We have already seen (in the last chapter) that Moses' focus was on what God had called him to do; it wasn't on any selfish desires of his own or on the demands of people who wanted to abandon God's plan.

Compare Moses to Aaron. Now I know that comparison is dangerous, and comparing siblings is something no parent should do. And although what follows might lead you to believe something different, I'm really not trying to throw Aaron under the bus.

That said, Moses' judgment (while not perfect) seems to have been consistently better than Aaron's. Read Numbers 12 for a mysterious interlude in which Aaron and Miriam (Moses' sister) criticize Moses for marrying a Cushite woman and comment rather petulantly, **"Has the Lord spoken only through Moses? Hasn't he spoken through us, too?"** (Numbers 12:2, NLT) Aaron was not immune to small-mindedness and petty jealousies, apparently. Nor was he prepared to withstand the demands of the crowd.

The inadequacy of Aaron's filter shows up more than once in the story of Israel, perhaps most spectacularly when Moses disappears up a mountain for over a month, communing with God and receiving the Ten Commandments. Aaron, you'll remember, was charged with minding the store.

Faced with the same discontented voices Moses heard on an almost daily basis, Aaron didn't know what to do. So he caved to pressure and gave people exactly what they wanted: a new god (a cow) and a new leader (himself).

In a style that reflects a leader with a poor filter, Aaron defended his actions to Moses this way:

> **"Don't get so upset, my lord," Aaron replied. "You yourself know how evil these people are. They said to me, 'Make us gods who will lead us. We don't know what happened to this fellow Moses, who brought us here from the land of Egypt.' So I told them, 'Whoever has gold jewelry, take it off.' When they brought it to me, I simply threw it into the fire— and out came this calf!"** (Exodus 32:22-24, NLT)

I'm sure that's exactly what happened. Calves just form themselves.

THE DANGER OF HAVING NO FILTER

Moses knew what Aaron didn't:

Without a filter, everything sounds compelling.

There was at least some inherent logic to the ideas of return-
ing to Egypt, replacing Moses as leader (that comes up a few
times in the larger narrative), and giving up on God and His
plan for change. Aaron argued for all three at different points in
the journey. Moses didn't. Moses had a good filter. Aaron could
have used one.

The questions you use to form your filter can prove very helpful
as you lead people through change. Whichever questions you
decide are the best ones for your situation, know that having a set of questions that serve as a filter is critical, because
the questions you ask will shape the future you live. Just ask
Moses or Aaron.

TEST YOUR FILTER

Regardless of how attached you grow to your filter or how
helpful you think it might be, it's critical that you test it. If you
don't, you could completely mislead your team through a
season of change.

So how do you test your filter?

When it comes to testing filters, time is your ally. You can
test whether your filter is working once you get a few years
of leading change under your belt. The test is dead simple:
watch what happens when people leave your organization. If
the people you lose over time are indeed the kind of people
you cannot build the future of the church on, you'll know soon
enough. Some will stop attending church. Others, sadly, will go
to other churches and cause problems. Others will end up not
having much of an impact in the wider community. If your filter

weeds out those kinds of people, it might be a reasonably useful guide as to WHICH VOICES TO LISTEN TO[5].

If, however, the people who leave your organization end up at another church or in various other churches and are leading the way, making an impact, and are really advancing the mission elsewhere, you probably have a bad filter. You've developed a filter that strains out great leaders. And that's not good. I've seen this happen. And that's a place no one wants to be. If that happens, it's time to sit down with some trusted and wise leaders and try to figure out where the problem is.

Another word on testing your filter: insecure leaders will often assume that everyone who is opposed to them is the kind of person on whom you can't build the future of the church. They feel threatened by even the slightest disagreement with their idea of where things should move. If you feel some insecurity (and who doesn't?), I strongly suggest that you develop a test for your filter.

If your definition of "success" in ministry is that the "good" people are only those who agree with you, you will lead a fairly lonely ministry. Great leaders will abandon you, and you will eventually be surrounded only by the sound of your own voice. Getting alignment is not the same as getting agreement. In the next book of this Change Trilogy, we'll look at how alignment and agreement interrelate. You can have an aligned organization without having full agreement on issues. In fact, you should never try to create an organization where everyone agrees with everything. But that is for another day. For now, just test your filter. Make sure it works and that your filter keeps great leaders in the game.

In the end, a good filter will help you and your leaders navigate the sea of voices you hear. Without one, everything sounds compelling. With a good filter, you'll keep people who are both passionate about creating a biblical community and are the kind of people you can build the future of the church on. So develop some questions that form your filter. The questions you ask will shape the future you live.

📹 **For a Bonus Video, go to LeadingChangeWithoutLosingIt.com and click on "Quick Tip: Finding a Filter."**

STRATEGY

ATTACK PROBLEMS, NOT PEOPLE

STRATEGY 4

ATTACK PROBLEMS, NOT PEOPLE

Help people see you are for them even if you are not for their ideas.

LEADING CHANGE ... BUT LOSING IT

Ever really lose it in ministry? I remember one time when I lost it with someone in a congregational context. It happened about a decade ago, after the third and final weekend service in the school where we were meeting at the time. I was tired, and we had introduced drums in our band a few months earlier. A retired engineer in his eighties, whom I'll call Hal, was the last one of a long line of people to tell me the band was too loud that day. I smiled and was polite to everyone who went out of his or her way to tell me about it—until I saw Hal approach. He didn't say anything more drastic than anyone else. He was heated, but underneath was an earnestness and sincerity in his frustration. For some reason, he pushed the last unpushed button left inside me that day.

I still remember standing outside the doors to the school gym, leaning forward and telling him what I thought ... exactly what I thought. Raising my voice, I told him I didn't have a problem at all but that I was quite convinced he did. Making sure no sentiment was left unspoken, I also informed him that if he didn't like it, he should just get over it and maybe find another church that wasn't as loud, and I could help him do that.

Like all revenge, the satisfaction lasted about one second. Almost as soon as the words were out of my mouth, I was mortified. I went to his house that afternoon, utterly ashamed, and apologized. I then called all of our elders and told them what I had done. I felt terrible. At one point I thought I should probably resign, I was that sick over it.

As bad as that incident was, that wasn't my usual public pattern. In over 15 years of ministry, that time with Hal was the only time I've lost it publicly with people. Because my usual disposition was so measured, people would come up after difficult congregational events and ask how I had kept my cool. Truthfully, I'm not sure how I did it. I just did it.

When someone attacks you or your ideas, it's hard not to get defensive, or even not to counter-attack. There is something hardwired in our brains that makes us want to fight back. You threaten me and I push back, as though life were some kind of wicked gangster movie or as though we lived in the bush amidst hungry grizzlies (note that I am against both camping and gangsters, in that order).

Some of that fight instinct is healthy and necessary. It's part of being human. But it's not a particularly helpful skill if you are trying to navigate change, especially if you are trying to navigate change in a Christian context as a Christian leader.

Even though I had a pretty even external disposition (except for that day with Hal), I was doing a slow burn as a leader. I didn't really see a safe place to take my frustration, anger, and growing resentment. My problem wasn't that I usually attacked people in public; my problem was that I let the attack simmer internally. My outer demeanor was different from my private thought life. And in my mind on the car ride home or while mowing the lawn, I'd mull things over and get angry with people who differed from me. I'd attack them in my mind. Then I'd put my church face back on the next day and head to the office.

Sound familiar?

What do you do with your frustration? I mean, you know what happens to people who keep their frustrations stuffed deep inside, right? They either explode one day, or the opposite happens and their anger freezes what's left of their souls. Unresolved anger ends up surfacing in innocuous meetings over a $75 budget line item. You dig in and with all the sophistication of a toddler whose toy tractor was taken away, you decide to fight everyone to the finish on why you're entitled to $175, not $75. You behave like a pit bull in a room full of poodles. Or, if your anger doesn't erupt explosively like that, it will turn inward and slowly deaden your resolve. You walk into the meeting and see the $75 line item, but realize you are indifferent to whether you've been allotted $75 or $750,000. You step back and realize that you are actually uninterested in everything. The problem is not only that your passion is gone, it's that you don't know how to get it back.

Unresolved tension and anger are deadly. But you can't attack people. So what do you do? Enter Moses.

IF YOU DON'T TURN TO GOD …

Moses understood leaders need a place to vent. Frustrated with the perpetual complaints of hundreds of thousands of people in the desert (let that sink in for a minute next time you think your congregation or team complains), Moses got more than a little agitated. When his frustration rose, notice what Moses did with it. It would have been so tempting to assassinate the complainers verbally. But he didn't. Instead, Moses went directly to God. Let's jump back to Numbers 11:

> Moses heard all the families standing in the doorways of their tents whining, and the Lord became extremely angry. Moses was also very aggravated. And Moses said to the Lord, "Why are you treating me, your servant, so harshly? Have mercy on me! What did I do to deserve the burden of all these people? Did I give birth to them? Did I bring them into the world? Why did you tell me to carry them in my arms like a mother carries a nursing baby? How can I carry them to the land you swore to give their ancestors? Where am I supposed to get meat for all these people? They keep whining to me, saying, 'Give us meat to eat!' I can't carry all these people by myself! The load is far too heavy! If this is how you intend to treat me, just go ahead and kill me. Do me a favor and spare me this misery!" (Numbers 11:10-15, NLT)

Is there any church leader who can't relate to that? Seriously. As a leader, you've been aggravated, very aggravated. You've felt like the victim. You've blamed God—maybe even accused Him of tricking you into answering a call. You've complained about not having enough support, and you may have asked God to smite you. You might have even done all this at once after a particularly exasperating day.

But don't miss this: what Moses *says* is less important than what Moses *does*. Did you see what he did? Moses took it to God. He took his raw fury and let God have it.

Ever done that? For years, I thought it was illegal to do that. I thought prayers had to be manicured, like English hedges. But then I read the Bible. Passages like Numbers 11 at first shocked me, then amused me, and then became soul food. They also gave me permission to begin to pray more honestly.

I realize there might be resistance to this idea that you can let God "have it" with your frustrations, but if you think Moses crossed a line, I encourage you to read the Psalms and see what they're really saying. If you are looking for a particularly honest Psalm, try Psalm 109. In it, David said things that would get almost anyone thrown out of church today: he not only wished harm on his enemies, he wished them, their wives, their children, and their children's children dead. Have you ever paid close attention to what he said to God?

> May his [my enemy's] children wander as beggars
>> and be driven from their ruined homes.
> May creditors seize his entire estate,
>> and strangers take all he has earned.
> Let no one be kind to him;
>> let no one pity his fatherless children.
> May all his offspring die.
>> May his family name be blotted out in a single generation. (Psalm 109:10-13, NLT)

Those verses have probably not been embroidered and hung on your grandmother's wall, but they're as much a part of Scripture as the 23rd Psalm. There is much more to this passage than what I've quoted here if you care to read it. Just open your Bible.

While my prayer has never been quite as visceral as David's (maybe it should be), the point is well taken. Moses and David knew this about themselves when facing opposition:

If you don't turn to God, you'll turn on them.

Wisely, they turned to God. They told Him what they couldn't and shouldn't have told the people who hurt them, and somehow in the midst of it—or maybe because of it—they were able to lead. In fact, in the midst of intense opposition, these leaders learned how to lead nations. Instead of attacking people, they attacked problems.

SEPARATE THE PEOPLE FROM THE PROBLEM

This principle is so powerful, it's echoed in our culture. I saw this before I went into ministry, when I trained in law. A classic book used by many lawyers, William Fischer and Roger Ury's *GETTING TO YES*[6], states the principle this way: separate the people from the problem. This is a critical component of effective negotiation. Even the law recognizes what Moses and David knew as leaders: it is almost impossible to get movement and momentum on an issue if you are attacking people.

The principle reaches deeper than that though. Attacking the problem at hand actually allows you to build alliances. It creates common ground and helps you accomplish what you set out to do. People rally around leaders who are committed to solving problems.

Many of us would love it if elected officials actually wrestled down major issues facing our countries and the world. We quietly cheer when a new boss solves problems that no one else had the courage to address. We admire it when a friend decides to (lovingly) rebuke a business colleague whose moral compass has gotten confused. Attacking problems is a sign of great leadership.

Leaders who attack people rather than problems are a very different breed. They can leave a trail of bodies in their wake. Even if the people who leave your church don't have a biblical argument in what they are saying and are not the kind of people you are going to build the future of the church on, they don't need to walk away bleeding and limping. Even if you see a group of people as a problem, it's important to remember that people are ultimately a big part of the solution to any problem you face. The leader who stands alone doesn't stand for much in the end. If you treat Opponents poorly, it can leave everyone feeling insecure: "If you turned on *them* like that," they wonder, "are you going to turn on me in the same way if we disagree?" Addressing Opponents with grace, humility, and love is the best way to treat them.

Attacking problems instead of people also happens to be deeply consistent with the Christian faith. The Bible describes a God who goes to great lengths to deal with sin but rescue sinners. It chronicles a God who, despite the incredible problem of human depravity, loves the world.

FOUR WAYS TO AVOID ATTACKING PEOPLE

So how do you affirm people while attacking the problem? It's easier said than done, but several learnable practices can be very helpful. Given that the rest of the book is about tackling the problem of change, we might want to drill down on how to avoid attacking people for a few moments.

What follows are some practical tips that can help you in the heat of everyday interaction with Opponents in everything from emails to phone conversations to spontaneous encounters (in the foyer or the supermarket) to formal congregational meetings. As we've seen from both Moses and David, being able to speak honestly with God about it is a necessary foundation. But there are also some other practical skills that can help save the moment and the momentum you've built when it comes to change. I've found these four practical strategies have helped me keep my composure in the moment even when my emotions impel me in other directions.

1. Believe the best. There may be some people who are out to harm you, but most people aren't. They are just sincerely doing what they believe is best for the future. Their vision just conflicts with yours and that of your team.

It is so easy for me to impute bad motives where none exists. Although it doesn't appear to most people that I have a thin skin, I have a bad habit of taking non-personal things personally. My family still has to remind me of this sometimes. In my early days of leadership, I assumed that if someone was threatening the vision we were advancing, they were somehow against me. I was ascribing a motive to them they almost never had. The more I'm able to believe the best about other people—especially people who disagree with me—the better leader (and person) I become. It allows me to separate the person from the problem and attack the problem, not the person.

So I've learned to think that someone who has a very different understanding of the future is really imagining what they believe to be a better future. I'm also learning to assume that what they believe makes perfect sense to them, even if it doesn't make perfect sense to me.

And somehow, when I do that, not only do I not take things as personally, I'm able to better see and address the issues. It also reminds me that I might be wrong, and that helps me keep a more humble attitude.

They also happen to be people who share the same Savior, same faith, and ultimately, the same heaven. So why wouldn't I treat them with respect, regardless of how they treat me? Jesus said something about blessing your enemies. You will never look back with regret if you remain generous and kind to people who are not kind to you. And one of the best ways I know of to ensure you do that systematically is to begin by assuming the best of others, not the worst.

> 🎬 **To hear more, click on**
> **"You Are Not the Kingdom,"**
> **at LeadingChangeWithoutLosingIt.com.**

2. Empathize with your Opponents. Believing the best is about what happens in your mind when you realize there is opposition. Showing empathy is a practice you can adopt when you open your mouth. It's natural not to want to show empathy toward those who disagree with you. In fact, my instinct is to lack empathy for people with differing views. I want to dismiss them, discount them, counter them, or even belittle them (on bad days). Don't. Instead, show empathy toward them. Instead of beginning a conversation by stating your differences, why not begin by emphasizing what you both agree on and trying to understand why your "opponent" is upset? For example, instead of saying:

> *Josh, you and I completely disagree and I'm not sure there's anything we can do about it. I just can't see it your way and you can't see it my way.*

... why not say something like this:

> *Josh, I'm grateful we share a commitment to Christ as our Lord. And I'm thankful for what you're doing to help us try to advance our mission. I sense that you're upset with the direction we're heading in. I just want you to know I understand that, and I hope we can discuss our differences.*

Do you hear the difference? I think if you or I were on the other side of the changes in an organization, we'd want a leader to approach us with the second attitude, not the first.

When you show empathy, you help people understand that they were heard. And that's huge. Sometimes that's all people want. In some ways, this is exactly like the dynamic between many husbands and their wives. It took me about a decade and a half of marriage to figure out that when my wife, Toni, started sharing her struggles with me, she didn't want me to solve them. I could usually solve her problem in minutes (or at least in my mind I had solved it in minutes). For 15 years it floored me (I'm slow to pick up on patterns) that she resisted my wildly brilliant solutions. Then one day it dawned on me: she just wanted me to listen. She was looking for empathy. While it still seems utterly strange to me for someone to share a problem and not want a solution, I now listen intently and say things like "I understand" and "That's too bad" and "I get that" and at the end of the discussion, she actually feels better. I still feel puzzled, but I promise you it works.

If you can empathize with the people who oppose you, you will de-escalate the relational tension. In fact, you'll discover that after being heard, some (not all) Opponents will change their minds and even support the proposal at hand. They just wanted to know that you understood and heard them. When I apologized to Hal and his wife that day, they treated me with empathy and understanding. In fact, they took the journey with us into our new building and helped us welcome hundreds of new people we never would have reached had we not embraced change. Sadly, Hal and his wife have both since passed away, but we were on good terms when he died. That's the power of empathy. He showed it to me, and despite my outburst that day, I'm learning to better show it to others.

3. Wait a day. No matter how mature we become, we all have emotional reactions to things. You really wouldn't want others to hear your instinctive reaction when the guy with a fish symbol on the tailgate of his truck cuts you off in rush hour traffic, would you? Probably not. The instinct might never go away on this side of heaven, but that doesn't excuse you from acting on those instincts. I've always thought of it this way: I'm not responsible for what I feel, but I am responsible for what I say and do.

Which is why I've found it so helpful not to act on my emotions when in the midst of conflict. I'm going to feel things in conversations and when I read correspondence. But I don't have to tell everyone what I'm feeling, and I don't need to react emotionally. The longer I wait when responding to something that frustrates or angers me, the better I do in responding maturely.

A number of years ago I developed something I simply call my "24-hour rule." The rule is this: if I read something or hear something that upsets me emotionally, I promise myself not to respond to it for at least 24 hours. Now, you can't always follow that in a meeting or conversation, but it's surprising how often you can wait 24 hours to respond to just about everything else. (In fact, while you may need to continue the conversation or finish the meeting, you don't have to respond to the matter that provoked you most. You can wait until the next day to follow up on the most emotional issue.) You can always follow the 24-hour rule with emails, voice mail, and direct messages. I find that by the next day, I no longer want to say some of the things I wanted to say when I first read what they wrote or picked up the voicemail. I find the 24-hour rule so helpful that any time something evokes a negative emotional response in me (you know, that feeling in your stomach as you're reading/hearing what they have to say), I wait a day.

4. Reply relationally. Face it: people can get nasty behind a keyboard. We say things we would never say in person and often send them before sober second thought sets in or before someone stands over our shoulder and says, "You're not actually going to send that, are you?" Apparently we are. And we do.

We've all been on the receiving end of those kinds of blasts. So what do you do after you've calmed down, or even waited a day? Waiting a day doesn't mean you won't be upset anymore—it just means you'll be rational.

Here's a strategy that can really help. Reply relationally. Make sure your response is more relationally direct than their complaint was. If you get a letter (do people still send letters?), an email, or a direct message, pick up the phone and call them back. If you get a voice mail, call them back and offer to meet them for coffee.

When you call them or offer to meet with them, you will surprise them and disarm them. They weren't even sure you read the message and are already a bit surprised you didn't just hit delete. But what's equally surprising is that you didn't follow suit. You didn't just sit behind your keyboard and blast back. You engaged them. When you do so in a way that follows the other practices we've outlined in this chapter, you'll find that most of the time the conflict de-escalates. Sometimes it even disappears. Even if it doesn't, you have the peace of mind knowing that you handled things in the best way you could.

THE HIGH ROAD IS THE BEST ROAD

There is no guarantee that the methods described in this chapter will work, but often you'll find these practices can significantly reduce conflict. Beyond that, it will help you know that as a leader, you conducted yourself with integrity. You did everything you could to treat people fairly and with dignity. Years from now, you'll be so glad you did.

The high road is the hard road, but it's also the best road. There are many reasons for this, but here's one we can almost all relate to. At some point, you'll be in the supermarket and you'll encounter the person who wrote you a nasty note or crashed your congregational meeting. How you conducted yourself when you were in the midst of the battle will determine whether you meet that person with a smile, endure a really awkward moment, or even pretend you didn't see them and move to the next aisle. You might not end up vacationing together in the future, but that's not the point. The point is you will have conducted yourself with integrity and in a way that others will see as admirable. And you will have attacked a problem, not a person. The kingdom could use much more of that.

For a Bonus Video, go to LeadingChangeWithoutLosingIt.com and click on "Quick Tip: Attacking Problems, Not People."

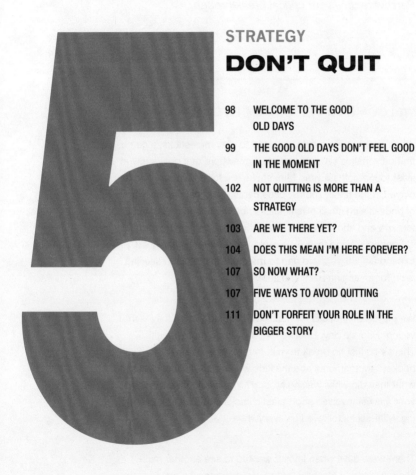

STRATEGY

DON'T QUIT

STRATEGY 5

DON'T QUIT

Persevere until your critical breakthrough.

WELCOME TO THE GOOD OLD DAYS

When my sons were little, we used to play mini-sticks, a game that only makes sense if you live somewhere that gets snow at least four months a year. Mini-sticks is a form of indoor hockey played in the family rooms, basements, garages, and hallways of houses with small plastic sticks not much longer than your forearm and about as wide as a school ruler. In other words, it's perfectly sized for a 6-year-old—and perfectly designed to send any 36-year-old dad to the medicine cabinet, seeking relief for an aching back and shoulders.

We played mini-sticks for hours with our kids when they were young. Hours a day. Hours every day, to be more specific. There was just no break from it. In fact, when we went to "real hockey" tournaments and the kids weren't on the ice, guess what they did while waiting around? You would be correct if your answer involved short plastic sticks and a lot of screaming. Mini-sticks followed us everywhere.

There were days when I never wanted to see another mini-stick. At times, I gleefully traded with anyone who would play even one hour with my boys because I had a debilitating case of mini-stickitis. But for the most part, even though I wanted to quit, I didn't. And now I'm glad I persevered through that phase.

Those days are gone (it's been almost seven years since we last played mini-sticks), but I will forever remember those seemingly endless hours of torture. Only now, I smile about them. So do my kids. For them and for me, those moments became part of what we think of as "the good old days." The time put in on mini-sticks (even against my will some days) forged a deeper and better relationship with both my sons that we're still enjoying to this day.

Believe it or not, the same will be true for you if you're currently in the midst of difficult change. The challenges you're facing right now are moments you will one day look back on as the good old days—provided you don't quit before you break through. Sure, there will be moments far more painful and searing than those parents suffer through mini-sticks, but the principle isn't that different.

THE GOOD OLD DAYS DON'T FEEL GOOD IN THE MOMENT

When I reminisce with others about the change our church navigated, we look back on it and say things like:

- Remember the day we had no musicians and I had to lead worship? (I'm surprised the church didn't close for good that Sunday.)

- Remember that first year when we had an average attendance of six at one of our campuses? (As mentioned earlier, we started with three small churches who couldn't afford a "real" pastor, and each congregation met in its own building.)

- Remember that meeting where 75% of the people actually voted in favor of selling all three historic buildings? (Only God could have brought about that result.)

- Remember our first day in the elementary school wondering if anyone would show up?

- Remember how, during construction, we wrote the names of unchurched people on the stage floor and walls and prayed for them before the names were covered over?

- Remember that night the loan fell through and we realized we needed to raise $500,000 in two weeks or we couldn't open our doors?

I assure you there were more than a few tense moments behind those memories. Actually, the last story hinted at above was a particularly powerful occasion. Sometimes the opposition isn't someone who doesn't like an idea, but external factors that seem to conspire against you.

When we were starting Connexus Church, we had arranged an outside start-up loan for $500,000. It was going to help us pay for all our gear for portable church. One Tuesday, I got the call that the lender had changed his mind. With the loan gone, I immediately called some of our key leaders together. We didn't even sit around a table that night. We sat down together on the floor, utterly dejected, as the shock of losing our start-up funding set in. It was a very tough season. We were in the process of exiting the denomination we had been a part of until that point. The criticism we faced on that alone had been intense and prolonged. The loan was the only money we had to launch the new church. We didn't even have a bank account set up at that point and had zero dollars raised toward the launch. The loss of the loan felt like an almost fatal blow. I told them, "I feel like Moses standing on the shore of the Red Sea. God has got to part some waters here because otherwise, we are either going to get slaughtered by the Egyptians or drown, and right now I don't know which it will be." Not exactly a rousing speech, but it's pretty much verbatim what I said. It's not that I really wanted to quit that night, but it began to look like it was the only option.

Remarkably, God was ready to part some water. Deciding not to die to the dream we believe God gave us (to transition to a church unchurched people would love to attend), a handful of us called everyone we knew who wanted to be part of this venture, told them what happened, set up a bank account, and asked them to give. Ten days later we had raised over $550,000. Half a million dollars in ten days. We didn't even have our charitable status as a church yet, so there were no guarantees anyone was going to get a tax receipt. Even now, I can still hardly believe that actually happened. And I am still so thankful for it.

That bit of history illustrates something I have come to realize on more than a few occasions: we are often most tempted to quit or give up moments before our critical breakthrough. We put in the work, doing everything we can to execute the plan faithfully, until we reach the point where it just isn't enough. It seems there is nothing else to be done. And we're tempted to give in and call it quits. But when we persevere beyond our natural strength and endurance, we hand the pen to God. We give God permission to write a story we can't write ourselves. And we discover what so many have discovered over time:

when you come to the end of yourself, you'll begin to see what God can do.

NOT QUITTING IS MORE THAN A STRATEGY

Navigating change is about making it to the end. If you quit before the breakthrough happens, transformation doesn't happen. If deep and revolutionary change were easy, everybody would be doing it. And they're not.

But there's a reward for those who do: *perseverance is actually part of the path of discipleship.* As we'll see in another volume of this Change Trilogy, if you look for biblical examples of the life we'd like to live as leaders (that of unmitigated success and great popular appeal), you won't find many. For example, Paul wrote his best stuff while in prison. And he wasn't in prison because of disobedience; he landed in jail because he was being faithful to his calling.

Paul called it a mark of spiritual growth: "We also rejoice in our sufferings, because we know that suffering produces perseverance; perseverance, character; and character, hope." (Romans 5:3-4, NIV) James told us to throw a little party every time we suffer and face trials, because it produces perseverance (James 1:2-3). You ever do that? Ever put up a morning Facebook post that says, "Suffering ahead today and I'm so grateful!!!!" Didn't think so. Me neither. The desire to avoid suffering and trials, even while engineering necessary change, may be human nature, but it isn't possible, and (according to Scripture) it's an immature way of looking at life.

If there is one piece of advice I have for leaders who are trying to navigate healthy, God-given, needed change, it's this: Don't quit. Persevere. And remember, you will be tempted to quit. In fact, you'll be most tempted to quit moments before your critical breakthrough.

ARE WE THERE YET?

I wonder if this is (often, not always) why many church leaders have short tenures. They arrive in a new ministry position, get to know people over the first year or two, and then encounter the demanding task of change. The leader builds momentum with the Early Adopters and Early Majority, but Opponents surface. It gets tough. And several years into the process of change, exasperated and exhausted, he or she throws in the towel before the transformation happens.

I personally don't believe there is a standard calendar for change. As for the specific change you have in mind, you might be able to engineer what you want to accomplish within a year; in other situations it might take a decade. The time it takes depends on the size of the challenge you're facing, the composition of the group you are leading, and your own leadership style. These three "ingredients" add to or lessen the time required accordingly.

While the timeline isn't bankable, some change theorists suggest that change can happen in three to five years, but transformation doesn't happen until the seventh year. The power in that idea is that change takes time, but true transformation takes even more time. Because of the time required to effect change and transformation, you are likely to be tempted to quit before your critical breakthrough.

Some people argue that not everyone is called to lead organizations through full seasons of change. Isn't it true that some are called to sow seed, some to cultivate, and some to reap? Absolutely! But what bothers me is that many leaders just sow and then go. Others leave when the cultivating gets tough. Few actually make it to the harvest. I'm not saying that's a mistake in every case, but I do wonder whether the trend among many leaders is to leave before the job is finished.

Maybe it comes down to this: as a leader you shouldn't value other peoples' opinions of yourself more than you value God's. Don't automatically head for the door when the voices of opposition to change become loud. Don't fool yourself into thinking your next ministry will just be "easier." That's kind of like saying your next wife/husband will be more understanding. You still bring "you" into every relationship you have, in the same way that you bring your undealt-with fears and frustrations into any ministry you will lead in the future.

📽 To hear more from Carey about
"How Long Will It Take?"
go to LeadingChangeWithoutLosingIt.com.

DOES THIS MEAN I'M HERE FOREVER?

So does this mean you're going to stay in your current ministry assignment forever? Probably not. God does call us on, but we need to make sure we're not leaving just because the pressure is too intense.

So what are some signs that maybe the battle is over and you should move on? When does the opposition become too much for you to stay in your current role?

I want to be careful here because none of this is designed to take the place of your hearing from God. But here are three conditions (there may be others) that, if true, would make me think twice about staying (or reconsidering the plan for change):

1. Your spouse thinks it's time to give in or move on. No one knows me better than my wife. I trust her judgment more than I trust my own in many issues. If she believes it's time to move on, I would at least take that to God (and to other counsel) for prayerful consideration. Those of us who are married realize that our spouses can usually see if our passion for God is waning to an unhealthy level over a long period of time. And while it's a delicate subject in marriage, spouses can probably also sense if we have both the gifting and the skill necessary for the change ahead of us. If we don't, they'll gently suggest it's time to move on. If you are not married, then you might ask a best friend, parent, or someone who knows you exceptionally well to give you this kind of feedback.

2. Your circle of wise counsel is unanimously telling you to reconsider. If you believe you are right, but you are pretty much the only one, it's a sign you might be wrong or that your vision isn't right for this group of people. If my inner circle told me I was pushing too hard for change, or the vision I was advancing was the wrong one, I would have to take that very, very seriously, and maybe realize I wasn't the right leader for this team. Or that I needed to think through my approach again. Similarly, they might see that my passion has waned below acceptable levels over time, or that I don't have the necessary gifting and skill for the challenges ahead. Leaders need to consider what wise counsel has to say.

3. You have lost the confidence of the most capable leaders in the organization. This one sounds similar to #2, but it's a little different. Essentially, this refers to the positional leaders in your organization. If I lost the confidence of our elders or leadership team, I would resign and move on. I would not only need to trust that God might be speaking through them, but I would also need to realize that my influence as a leader was gone. Without influence, you can't bring about change. If you lose the confidence of the most capable leaders, the current chapter of the story may indeed be ending.

The list above is not scientific. But if two or three of those conditions are true over a longer time period (say three to six months, minimum), it might be time to move on. If only one is true, or if it's only true for a short season, you might want to hang in there a bit longer. After all, even Moses lost the confidence of his closest leaders for a season. We all have bad days. We all have bad weeks. Some leaders might even have a bad year. But if the conditions above are true over time, they might be a sign God is indeed calling you to move on and your season of leadership in that organization is finished.

If that's true, that's not necessarily a sign that your leadership has been a failure. The best leaders will always seek to learn what they could have done differently and get input from a variety of voices about how they should have handled things. But failure to bring about change doesn't always mean you failed.

So why does change not always work out? Honestly, who really knows? But here are two possible reasons. First, the change might not fit God's timing. And second, God is in it, but perhaps He has a different leader in mind to lead the charge. Consider Moses. No matter how much he wanted to "persevere" into the Promised Land, God had a different leader in mind to finish the job (and yes, this was because of a specific act of disobedience on Moses' part; see Numbers 20:12-13). SOME OF US MIGHT BE MOSES, AND SOME OF US MIGHT BE JOSHUA[7].

SO NOW WHAT?

Assuming that none of those conditions has been met in your situation, how do you keep your heart and head in the game? How do you stay in leadership long enough to see the change realized?

To some extent, that's something you and God have to work out. Perseverance requires you and me to get on our knees and hammer out a relationship with Him that is deeply personal and relentlessly honest. It will require you to go places in prayer you never even knew existed. It will bring the Psalms to life and make them leap off the page. (Read Psalm 77 in the NLT. Yes, every BIBLICAL LEADER[8] you can think of went through a version of what you are going through.) Perseverance necessitates growth, but it won't be because you went to yet another con-ference. It will be because God broke you, and you are actually relying on His strength, not your own.

FIVE WAYS TO AVOID QUITTING

While leading change is an inherently personal and complex journey for every leader, there are practical, everyday things we can do that can help us get to the other side of a critical breakthrough. While this isn't an exhaustive list, here are five practices that have helped me persevere in leadership over the years. I hope they can help you:

1. Find friends. Many leaders are lonely. It happens for a variety of reasons, but in part it's a systems problem. We tend to develop "dual relationships" with people in our ministry setting. Sure, we have friends, but our friends also go to church with us, or volunteer with us, or set our salaries, or we are their leaders. Which means often we hold back in what we tell them about the struggles we are facing because, well, we don't want them to see "their" church through that filter. Alternatively, if we're completely open with them about our struggles, they may lose heart for the mission. They might even leave. The best practice I've seen, and also personally experienced, is to be intentional about developing a small network of trusted colleagues outside your community. I have developed friendships with leaders who live hundreds—even thousands—of miles away who know me and with whom I can be 100% honest. It's been life-changing. And I am that friend to some of them too. Finding someone outside your faith community (even if it's a pastor or staff member across town) can become a mutually beneficial relationship.

That said, *don't neglect local friendships.* They are necessary and make life so much more rewarding. I am fortunate to have a great relationship with our elders. They know me inside and out, all my strengths and weaknesses, and we work hard at cultivating those relationships. I also have a transparent relationship with our staff, especially with our leadership team. And naturally, we have some great friends in the church and outside the church locally too. It's the combination of great relationships inside the church and outside the church that can provide for great support through good and bad seasons for everyone.

2. Get some help. A decade ago I sat down with a counselor for the first time. Jim helped me get through some key issues, and he helped my wife, Toni, and me navigate some of the pitfalls common to couples when one is called into ministry.

I've seen a few counselors over the last decade during different seasons and am quite sure I wouldn't be in ministry today if it weren't for their influence in my life. When I've been tempted to quit moments before a key breakthrough, my wife, prayer, wise words from others, and the help of a counselor made all the difference. I really believe God uses other people to speak to us. Interestingly enough, I don't know of a single influential ministry leader who's made it over the long haul who hasn't been through some form of formal or informal counseling. My only question is why I didn't go sooner.

3. Create an encouragement file. A number of years ago, I began filing away emails, letters, notes, and correspondence that encouraged me. It started with an actual file folder, but these days it's a virtual folder in my email client. My criteria for putting a note in the file: *Did the note make me feel like I'm making a difference?* It might be from someone who wrote to say thanks, or a colleague who Tweeted or Facebooked some encouragement, or an email from someone at our church who liked something that happened. Basically, if something encourages me, even in a small way, and helps me see God is using my efforts (because often it's easy to feel like He's not), I file it. I do it because, like you, one negative email can erase the memory of a hundred positive ones. I also keep it because on the days that I get discouraged, I know I can open that file and find hundreds of reasons to keep going. Ironically, when I feel discouraged, I usually don't even need to read a single note. Simply knowing they are there reminds me to keep going. Don't have an encouragement file? Start one today.

4. Find something energizing to occupy your time off. The problem with leadership in ministry is that it's hard to turn it off. Even when I'm not "working" I'm always thinking: about how to solve the next problem, how to develop a team member, what to teach in our next series, or how to navigate the next change.

I don't have a good "off switch." Most leaders I know don't have one.

One of the best ways to combat this is to develop something—a hobby, a pastime, or a pursuit—that energizes you. I didn't have one for years and finally decided to take up cycling. I thrive on it. My wife and I also hike, and we love to travel. I have other friends who have picked up photography, marathon running, and even video-gaming as pursuits that give them energy when they are away from the office. If your off time is always just down time, you will feel down. Your mind won't turn off. You need something to get your mind off the pressure of leadership. If you can find some energizing pursuits (even making time for dinner with friends who are life-giving), you will bring more energy to your work, a new perspective to your challenges when you get back to the office, and have more staying power over the long haul.

5. Develop a devotional life that has little to do with work.
Last year, I asked our staff a tough question: If none of us could do ministry tomorrow, what would be left of our spiritual lives? That's such an important question for leaders to ask, and when I've asked it of other leaders on the road, the answers haven't always been encouraging. I push myself and our leaders hard on developing a spiritual walk that has little to do with our work. Over a decade ago, I started reading *The One Year Bible* every year, not because there's magic to reading the entire Bible annually, but because I wanted to make sure my devotional life wasn't just more prep for Sunday. While I pray for others and our ministry, I want to make sure that my prayer life is rich enough to be meaningful if I stopped doing ministry tomorrow. Interestingly, acting as though you weren't in ministry when it comes to your spiritual walk might make it easier for you to stay fresh in ministry over the long run.

You may develop your own practices that keep you healthy over the long haul. By all means—whatever you need to do to stay healthy in the long run, do it! Prioritize it. You can only bring to others what you have experienced yourself.

DON'T FORFEIT YOUR ROLE IN THE BIGGER STORY

Whether you serve in several ministries or roles over your life, or whether you stay in one place for decades, I believe you are called to persevere and engineer the change this generation needs.

When you quit before your critical breakthrough, something very personal is at stake. God is going to do what God is going to do no matter what. But He's invited you to play a role in it. If you quit before God releases you, you forfeit your role in the bigger story.

There have been moments—more than a few moments—when I wanted to quit. In my worst moments, my ambition is to work at a place like Walmart and stack boxes. It sounds so appealing because when you move boxes, they stay stacked. In ministry, nothing ever seems to stay "stacked." You think you've got buy-in, only to go to the next meeting and realize you're three steps behind where you thought you were. I think that's why I like to mow the lawn so much. I start with a "problem" (the grass is long) and an hour later I've solved it (the grass isn't long anymore, and the diamond cut looks awesome). Ministry isn't like that.

So sometimes I fantasize about an escape from ministry that would allow me to pursue something "normal" with half or even a quarter of the pressure.

But then I realize God called me here for a reason. Truthfully, I don't know what story He's writing, but I do know this. He invited me into a role. Even a small role. And looking back on it one day decades from now, I think I'll be glad I didn't forfeit my role in the story. He can make me play any role He wants, but I'm so thankful God has given me even a small role to play. And He's given you one too.

Imagine you're Moses. You have no idea where all of this is heading. And you don't know exactly what your role is, but many days you wish your role was sheepherder like it was before. It was so easy. Sheep are far less complicated than people, or exoduses.

Imagine that you're feeling what Moses was feeling. (You might even re-read Numbers, chapters 11, 12, and 14, now.) Imagine what it's like to have even your brother and sister turn on you for a moment. Imagine what it's like to have people call for your resignation almost daily. Imagine what it's like to trek with a group, whose key disposition is ingratitude, across a scalding/freezing desert for four decades.

While it would take a while—and even Moses wouldn't see the Promised Land personally—a breakthrough for his people was coming. They were already free, but they were about to become the people through whom all humanity would be redeemed.

In fact, you're a Christian in part because Moses persevered. From Moses' perseverance came a nation, and from that nation came a Savior who redeemed every nation. You have faith, and your children have faith, because Moses kept going. Would God have found another way to save His people and usher in the salvation Jesus brings? Of course He would have. But Moses got to be part of the story. And so, in our own small way, do you and I.

If you quit, you'll forfeit your role in the bigger story.

YOUR ROLE IN STORY

Not quitting before our critical breakthrough gives us the privilege of being part of a bigger story God is writing. And He is inviting you to be a part of something that's much bigger than you or I realize.

🎬 **For a Bonus Video, go to LeadingChangeWithoutLosingIt.com and click on "Quick Tip: Not Quitting."**

IN CLOSE

IT ALL STARTS WITH A DREAM

Everything starts with a dream.

One of my dreams as a kid was to learn more about radio. I always loved music and was captivated by broadcasting. I used to listen to hours and hours of radio a day as a kid and was fascinated by what it would be like to work in radio. So when I was 16 I walked into the local radio station and asked them to hire me. They did.

Even as a teenager, I was intrigued by how to program a show so listeners would tune in to it. I created a Top 40 show for the local station and got to play all the songs I loved. All this happened while I was still attending our local church in my hometown.

Our church had great teaching but the service itself was very traditional. Contemporary meant you rolled out a piano for a Gospel hymn. I was attending, but most of my friends were not. I knew they needed to hear the message, but the service itself seemed to be driving people under 30 (or maybe 50) away. Radio then (like the music industry now) was pushing the cultural envelope.

One day I was driving down the road listening to the station I worked for. For the first time the two worlds in my life collided and I thought, "What if we just played music that sounded like *that* in church?" I realize now that that wasn't a new idea. But in the late 1980s I had never heard of Bill Hybels or Willow Creek or that student pastors across the nation were reinventing church. All I knew was organs, choirs, and Gospel pianos.

When I began ministry in those first three churches, they were much smaller versions of the church I grew up in. I had no idea whether we would be able to pull off a transition, but I knew we needed to try. I had realized by then that thousands of churches were making the transition to new styles of worship and new ways of being the church. We needed to become part of a larger movement of churches that was trying new things to reach outsiders other churches weren't reaching.

It still makes me thankful most Sundays to think that we actually have an incredible band that sounds like anything you could download off a chart on iTunes—sometimes even better. While we can debate models and ways to be the church (attractional, missional, organic, blended, etc.), what excites me is we've found something that's working in our communities. As I hope you find as well.

It's not about people's musical taste nearly as much as it is that the church is now home to hundreds of families who thought church wasn't for them. In fact, over half of the growth God has given us at Connexus is from families that had no pattern of regular church attendance before a friend invited them to a Sunday morning. The incredible music is one of the things that brings people back, which in turn leads them to connect in community, to surrender their lives to Christ, to be baptized, and ultimately to serve, give, and invite some of their friends to experience the same thing they experienced. God is changing lives.

The primary way we connect relationally at our church is through community groups. The small group we joined within two years of launching Connexus had 12 members. When it started, only a few of us in the group would have described ourselves as Christ-followers. Most of the group had all been invited by friends to Connexus over the first year. One of them had been raised in the home of an atheist, and she and her husband had zero church in their background. Another couple had let church drift off their radar screen for a decade or more. Another was curious and wanted to know more.

That group was an incredible journey. By the end of our two years together as a group, several people had made life-changing decisions to follow Christ. Three were baptized. In one family, all three of their teenage kids made decisions to follow Jesus as Savior. It's an exceptional story that God is still writing and it's not close to being over.

JUST HOW EASY IS IT TO RAISE THE DEAD?

The challenge in the North American church now is that many churches that are finding success in reaching people are new church plants. Now don't get me wrong; I love church planters and new churches (in fact, that's kind of what we have in Connexus). But the vast majority of churches are existing churches that need to change. Sure, church plants are navigating change within a year or two of launch, but existing churches have a significant battle ahead of them.

In 1999, four years into our time at the original three churches, my wife and I went to a church conference in North Carolina. We learned some things about reaching unchurched people and making a difference in a community that were absolute catalysts in our journey. It was mostly church planters in the room, but we were among the handful of people from existing congregations.

During a break, Toni and I took a minute to talk to one of the speakers. We told him about our situation and that we were trying to bring about change in three small, struggling mainline churches. I'll never forget what he said. He looked at us and replied:

> "You're trying to do that in three mainline churches? I've never seen that work. Ever. Listen, it's far easier to give birth than it is to raise the dead."

I don't think he was trying to be discouraging; he was just naming a reality that existed over a decade ago. Those of us in leadership need to change that reality. We really do.

There are church leaders across North America who are transitioning existing churches to become as relevant to this generation as those churches were to generations decades or centuries ago. It calls for a courageous and humble leadership that is committed to a vision for what could be, not for what is.

A GOD WHO RAISES THE DEAD

Just a few days ago, we held a celebration night for our church we simply call "Grateful." We do this every once in a while to facilitate some incredible worship, share communion, celebrate what God is doing, and thank the volunteers and donors who make it possible.

At the end of the night, we placed a large puzzle on stage. We invited everyone to come forward and take a piece of the puzzle. We wanted them to know that they played an indispensible part of the story God is writing and that what they're doing is making a difference.

The picture on the puzzle was a photo of my friend Anita, from my community group, being baptized. Dreams do come true. That was a dream for her, for our group, and for the kind of church we had hoped to become.

A few minutes before we revealed the picture on the puzzle, I had preached on Romans 4:17 which simply says:

> **Abraham believed in the God who brings the dead back to life and who creates new things out of nothing.** (Romans 4:17, NLT)

Our God is indeed a God who brings the dead back to life, and creates new things out of nothing.

You don't need to die to your dream, because God hasn't died to His.

For more Bonus Videos, go to LeadingChangeWithoutLosingIt.com and click on the ones marked "Q&A."

NOTES

PREFACE

* This book is part of The Change Trilogy, a series of books about leading change in the face of opposition; understanding and engineering change; and creating a culture of exponential change in your organization. The second and third books of the series are scheduled for release within the next year.

INTRO

* See note above, about The Change Trilogy.

1 "Forced Out: Pastors' Fight and Flight," *Christianity Today*, May 9, 2012, http://www.christianitytoday.com/ct/2012/may/spotlight-may12.html?tab=read.

STRATEGY 1

2 One of the most widely cited studies of how the population adapts to change is by Everett M. Rogers. He identified the categories as follows: Innovators, 2.5%; Early Adopters, 13.5%; Early Majority, 34%; Late Majority, 34%; and Laggards, 16%. See Everett M. Rogers, *Diffusion of Innovations* (New York: Simon & Schuster, 1962, 1971, 1983, 1995, 2003). I've amalgamated and amended some of his categories for the purpose of this book, but the trends are reflected in our analysis.

3 As for Charles, he went on to effectively lead another congregation nearby and then on to a position in the military. We remained (and remain) great friends, and God is now

using his ministry to make a significant difference nationally and internationally.

STRATEGY 2

4 Andy Stanley, Reggie Joiner, and Lane Jones talk about this in *The Seven Practices of Effective Ministry* (Sisters, Oregon: Multnomah, 2004, p. 139).

STRATEGY 3

5 I understand that this subject—leaving some people behind—is very difficult, especially for Christian ministry leaders. Dr. Henry Cloud's *Necessary Endings: The Employees, Businesses, and Relationships That All of Us Have to Give Up in Order to Move Forward* (New York: HarperCollins, 2010) is incredibly helpful on this subject.

STRATEGY 4

6 See Roger Fisher, William L. Ury, and Bruce Patton, *Getting to Yes: Negotiating Agreement Without Giving In* (New York: Penguin, 1991).

STRATEGY 5

7 My thanks to W. Scott Cochrane, Executive Director of Willow Creek Canada, for this insight on why change might not happen under your leadership.

8 Gene Edwards' powerful little book, *A Tale of Three Kings: A Study in Brokenness* (Carol Stream, Illinois: Tyndale House Publishers, 1992), is an eye-opening companion for the soul of leaders. It's a vivid account of the life of David, Saul, and Absalom that imagines the heart journey each of these leaders was on.

ACKNOWLEDGEMENTS

Change is never engineered by a single person; it takes a team to bring it about. The same is true for writing a book about change.

I would like to begin by expressing my gratitude to the people of the three small churches, the "originals" as we sometimes call them. They were part of the community long before my family and I showed up. Thank you for being willing to dream that tomorrow could be better than today, and thanks for putting your hearts on the line in deciding to reach out to a generation of unchurched people. You shouldered the opposition too, and it's a joy to continue to serve with many of you through all the seasons of change. I am so thankful for you, and there are many people over the years whose lives have been changed because of your courage.

I'm also grateful for those who took a very bold leap of faith almost five years ago to start Connexus Church. Your audacious faith and willingness to sacrifice much has already changed many lives that had never been impacted by church before. I hope you see what God is doing through you! I can't tell you what a privilege it is to serve with you and to be a part of a world-class team of leaders.

I also want to thank my family: my wife, Toni, and sons, Jordan and Sam. I hope you know there is no greater joy for me personally than spending time with you. The times we have together are the best I know. In addition, your constant support and encouragement is foundational to anything good that has happened, and I am a better person and better leader because of each of you. Your sacrifice over the years (even in supporting me through many evenings and weekends writing this book) is deeply appreciated.

A special word to Reggie Joiner: Reggie, I'm so thankful God brought our paths together a few years ago. From the moment we started hanging out, I realized that I not only had access to an exceptionally gifted leader of leaders, but that we had begun a deep friendship. Thank you for constantly encouraging me to get this material down in writing and to share it with leaders. Thanks for offering me a platform to publish it as well. It's a joy to be able to do this together. Your leadership and friendship is one of a kind.

At Connexus, Jeff Brodie and Sarah Flemming have been so helpful. Jeff provided all kinds of timely feedback, insight, and perspective that made the book better. Without Sarah's help as my assistant, my world would come to a screeching halt. As only Sarah can, she manages to keep a very busy world organized and on track, and does it with more grace than I ever could. Our staff team—Nadine, Jeff, Dan, Justin, Sarah, Andy, Jenn, Shawna, and Julia—are incredible to serve with. Our elders at Connexus have created a rare and much appreciated environment of support and friendship for the work at Connexus and special projects like this. So to our elders, three of whom are named David—John, Rob, David, Dave, and Dave—thank you for all you do to advance the mission here and in many other places.

As to the writing of this book, Melanie Williams at reThink has been an exceptional editor and coach in writing it. It's so much better because of your input! Brad Scholle, Kevin Benson, and Reggie Goodin's support of this project (as well as so many of my offbeat ideas) is deeply appreciated.

Reggie Joiner, Jeff Brodie, Casey Graham, Michael Lukaszewski, Ron Edmonson, Mike Jeffries, and W. Scott Cochrane read drafts of the manuscript and provided great suggestions and much appreciated encouragement along the way. Pete Wilson and Kara Powell have also offered some timely encouragement as we hit the home stretch of this book.

Casey Graham has become a good friend over the last year and half. We've grown really close quickly. Casey, your encouragement around this material has been so inspiring, and for you to believe in it and want it to have a great platform is so appreciated.

David McDaniel has been a big encourager of these (and other) ideas seeing the light of day. David, your friendship and support means so much.

And lastly, I want to thank Andy Stanley for giving me the opportunity to share some of these ideas in earlier forms at the Drive Conference, and for his belief in our team and our mission at Connexus as a North Point strategic partner. Andy, your insights and leadership are all over this book and all over my life. Thank you.

ABOUT THE AUTHOR

Carey Nieuwhof is the lead pastor of Connexus Community Church, a growing multi-campus church north of Toronto and strategic partner of North Point Community Church in Alpharetta, Georgia. Prior to starting Connexus in 2007, Carey served for 12 years in a mainline church, transitioning three small congregations into a single, rapidly growing congregation.

Photo by Chupp Photography

He speaks to North American and global church leaders about change, leadership, and parenting. Carey co-authored *Parenting Beyond Your Capacity* with Reggie Joiner.

Carey is a graduate of Osgoode Hall Law School (1991) and also holds degrees in history and theology. He was called to the Bar of Ontario in 1993 and then left law to pursue ministry.

He and his wife, Toni, live near Barrie, Ontario and have two sons, Jordan and Sam. In his spare time, you can find him cycling his heart out on a back road somewhere. He blogs at www.careynieuwhof.com and www.orangeparents.org.